California Coastal

Backcountry drives
for the
whole family

By **TONY HUEGEL**

Cover design, maps, art and production
by Jerry Painter

Photography by Tony Huegel

Published by The Post Company
P.O. Box 1800, Idaho Falls, Idaho 83403
(208) 522-1800

First edition
First printing June 1995
Second printing December 1996 (revised)

Produced in the United States of America.

Edited by Mei-Mei Chan & Dean Miller
Cover design and maps by Jerry Painter

Library of Congress Number 94-073983
ISBN 0-9636560-5-8

Cover photo: Punta Gorda, on the Lost Coast *(trip 9)*.

Disclaimer

This book was prepared to help you and your family enjoy backcountry driving. However, it is not intended to be an exhaustive, all-encompassing authority on backcountry driving, nor is it intended to be your only source of information about the subject. You must understand that there are risks and dangers that are inevitable when driving in the backcountry. If you drive the routes listed in this book, or any other backcountry roads, you assume all risks, dangers and liability that may result from your actions. The author and publisher of this book disclaim any and all liability for any injury, loss or damage that you, your passengers or your vehicle may incur.

Exercise the caution and good judgment that visiting the backcountry demands. Bring the proper supplies. Remember that the condition of backroads, especially those that are not paved, can and does change. Be prepared for accidents, injuries, breakdowns or other problems, because help is almost always far away.

Note: Winter rains along the coast often damage backcountry roads. Sometimes the damage is severe enough to warrant road closures of indefinite duration. Be sure to check with the appropriate agency on the condition of your chosen route before you set out.

Acknowledgments

No project of this sort stems from the effort of just one person. Some people helped by suggesting drives. Others helped by reading portions of the manuscript for accuracy and suggesting improvements. Still others made the whole thing possible in the first place.

Among the latter are my publisher, Jerry Brady, and my editor, Mei-Mei Chan.

No one's support and cooperation was more important or fundamental than that of my wife, Lynn MacAusland, and our children, Hannah and Land. They endured a lot while accompanying me during much of my research for this book. I couldn't be more grateful for their forbearance.

Also deserving of special thanks are Dean Miller and Jerry Painter, both of the Post Register newspaper in Idaho Falls, Idaho; Scott Sinclair of Six Rivers National Forest; Ron Woychak and Norm Noyes of Cleveland National Forest; and Gina Thompson of Los Padres National Forest. North Coast off-highway touring enthusiasts Patrick Lassiter and Dave Wheeler were also helpful.

Many others, including additional U.S. Forest Service and Bureau of Land Management personnel, as well as staffers in various county road departments, provided information that was vital to completing the book. I am grateful to them, too.

Contents

Locations of the drives

Crescent City
KLAMATH RANGES
Eureka
Lost Coast
NORTH COAST RANGES
N
5
SIERRA NEVADA MOUNTAINS
1
San Francisco
1
Big Sur
SOUTH COAST RANGES
101
Santa Barbara
TRANSVERSE RANGES
Los Angeles
CALIFORNIA DESERT
PENINSULAR RANGES
San Diego

Appendix

Route descriptions

Saying a coastal drive is fun, easy, hard, rough, long or short can be quite subjective. Much of that assessment depends on the individual's experience, likes and dislikes, perceptions and circumstances. I've tried to bring some objectivity to the various categories I've used to describe each drive, but that can only go so far. Here is what's behind each category:

LOCATION: Where the drive is.

HIGHLIGHTS: What's best about the drive.

DIFFICULTY: I've assumed you are not a hard-core four-wheeler, but just somebody in a modern sport-utility vehicle who's looking for reasonably safe adventure. The ratings, based on conditions in good weather, are: *easy*, which means it's a real cruise that won't require four-wheel drive; *moderate*, which means you may need four-wheel drive occasionally, the going will be slower, and you can expect occasional rough spots; and *difficult*, which means rough and slow, using four-wheel drive most of the time, and a higher likelihood that you'll scrape your undercarriage's protective skid plates on rocks once or twice. Some routes include places along the way that meet all three categories.

TIME & DISTANCE: The estimated time it takes to complete the drive, excluding your travel time getting to the starting point. The time element can vary enormously for each drive, depending on how much time you want to spend at stops along the way. Since odometer accuracy varies among vehicles, your measurements of distances might differ somewhat from mine. But they shouldn't differ much.

GETTING THERE: This will direct you to the starting point.

THE DRIVE: Details of the trip, such as what turns to take, where you'll end up, how far it is from here to there, and what you'll see along the way. You'll often see references to road numbers (13S01, for example) that the U.S. Forest Service assigns to roads in national forests.

REST STOPS: Where you can stop for a picnic, to camp, buy a bite to eat, explore a historic site, visit a museum, etc.

GETTING HOME: This will vary according to where home is. But there usually are common exit points leading to highways.

MAPS: Each route recommends a specific U.S. Forest Service map. I also recommend maps produced by the Automobile Club of Southern California (ACSC) and the California State Automobile Association (CSAA). They are free to members. There are many other good maps, as well. Shop around.

INFORMATION: The agency to contact for information about the route. Addresses and telephone numbers are listed under "Sources of information" beginning on page 144.

ALSO TRY: Other routes in the area that are not described in detail.

Map symbols

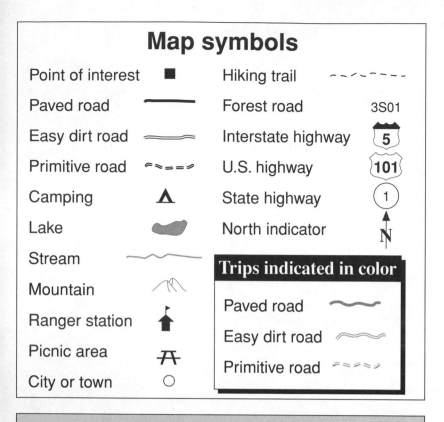

Point of interest	■	Hiking trail	- - ⁻ - - - -
Paved road	▬▬	Forest road	3S01
Easy dirt road	≈≈≈	Interstate highway	5
Primitive road	⌐≈==⌐	U.S. highway	101
Camping	▲	State highway	1
Lake	⬬	North indicator	N
Stream	～～		
Mountain	⌃⌃		
Ranger station	⬆		
Picnic area	⊼		
City or town	○		

Trips indicated in color

Paved road	～～
Easy dirt road	≈≈
Primitive road	⌐≈≈⌐

Guide for trip activities

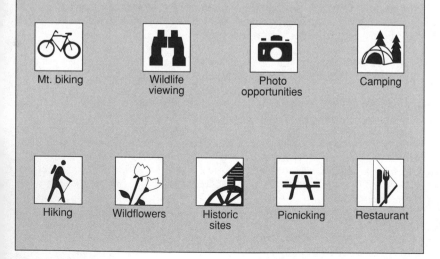

Mt. biking

Wildlife viewing

Photo opportunities

Camping

Hiking

Wildflowers

Historic sites

Picnicking

Restaurant

INTRODUCTION

The off-ramp to adventure

Escaping California's crowded highways, campgrounds and parks can often mean standing in line for a wilderness permit, hauling a backpack, praying that the next hill goes down instead of up and that the kids will understand that this is play, not punishment.

No more. With so many people switching from sedans, stations wagons and vans to more brawny and capable sport-utility vehicles, California's wild and uncrowded places are more accessible than ever before. Now families, maturing boomers, physically disabled people, seniors — just about anyone with a few hours to spare — can drive the state's huge network of adventure backroads to the kind of places that used to be the domain of hikers, mountain bikers and four-wheelers.

California Coastal Byways is your introduction to the unpaved alternatives in the spectacular mountain ranges between the Oregon border and the San Diego area. With a factory-stock SUV you'll be able to leave the highways and explore lush coastal forests, pastoral inland valleys and high ridges and peaks, places that relatively few people ever see. No longer will you have to wonder about those tantalizing little routes on your maps. This book will guide you to them, and tell you what you'll see along the way.

The routes I describe are either entirely unpaved, or substantially so. They range from well-graded dirt and gravel roads that are easy in two-wheel drive to more rugged two-track trails that can require the 4x4 capabilities built into your SUV. While some involve long detours from main highways and urban centers, others are just a short distance from major routes like Highway 1 and U.S. 101, and cities like Santa Barbara and Los Angeles. All are established roads open to public use. They are arranged essentially from north to south.

Choosing unpaved, often remote and rugged roads is much like choosing hiking trails instead of concrete sidewalks. They get us closer to nature and history, to what remains of California's wildlands, and to ourselves. They take us far from crowds, traffic and noise. They offer adventure, solitude, excitement and even challenges that help break up the routines of daily life.

California Coastal Byways tells you where to go, and how to get there and back safely while preserving the qualities that make unspoiled places worth visiting. You will also learn something about the geology as well as the natural and human history. Now and then I even mention good places to eat when you return to civilization.

With the help of *California Coastal Byways*, part of my series of guidebooks covering backcountry roads, you will discover a new side of a state that never runs out of surprises.

— *Tony Huegel*

Where land meets sea

When one thinks of California's justifiably famous coast, the images that come to mind most readily probably are those of the ocean crashing against the rocks at Big Sur, strolling along the Mendocino Headlands, sunbathing at Santa Cruz or catching a wave at Surfer's Point. But it is, of course, much more.

There is the region right next to the sea, and then there are the inland places. It includes trees of humbling size and age, cool breezes at the water's edge and searing heat just a few miles inland. It has soft hills of golden grass and oak woodlands not far from rain forests lush with ferns. One can sail in the bays, or stand atop ridges thousands of feet high and scan mountains that march from the sea to the desert. Some of America's greatest metropolitan areas — San Francisco, Los Angeles and San Diego — and their sprawling offspring are there. But so is the 60-mile strip of primitive coastline nicknamed the Lost Coast, the remotest, wildest and least populated segment of coast in California, and perhaps in the Lower 48. The Lost Coast includes the 66,000-acre King Range National Conservation Area, most of it proposed for federal wilderness protection, and the 7,367-acre Sinkyone Wilderness State Park. South of the Oregon border is forested Six Rivers National Forest. It includes the Smith River National Recreation Area, named for California's only undammed river. In the heavily populated south, just outside major urban and suburban areas, are Los Padres, Angeles and Cleveland national forests, which provide outdoor experiences for millions of visitors every year. These publicly owned wildlands encompass a number of federally protected wilderness areas. Among them is the 216,000-acre San Rafael Wilderness, which in 1968 became the first primitive area to be designated under the National Wilderness System.

California's coast includes mountains from four geologic provinces. Those provinces encompass 43 individual ranges. Many of these ranges lie far inland and are not considered coastal. Others are not considered coastal in geologic terms, but can still be part of the coastal experience. This complex jumble of mountains and valleys extends upwards of 1,000 miles from Oregon to Mexico along the curved western rump of the continent. This curvature is so great that coastal San Diego is farther east than Reno, Nev., in the Great Basin Desert.

According to the geologic theory of plate tectonics, two slabs, or plates, of the earth's shifting crust — the North American continental plate and the oceanic Pacific plate — had been slowly moving toward each other when they collided about 250 million years ago. The Pacific plate slipped, or subducted, beneath the continental plate, heating and melting as it reached the earth's super-hot interior. Between 140 million and 150 million years ago this molten rock, or magma, began to push upward. Thus were formed two of the four geologic provinces that include coastal mountains: the Klamath Ranges, which lie in the far north and extend into Oregon, and which contain some of the oldest rocks in North America; and the Peninsular Ranges, which stretch southward from the Los Angeles Basin to the tip of the Baja Peninsula.

About 25 million to 30 million years ago the movement of the two plates began to change, from head-on to slipping laterally against each other. This zone of slippage, which runs most of the state's length, is the

San Andreas Fault. As the Pacific plate moved northward and plunged beneath the North American plate, the latter scraped off sea floor sediments from the Pacific plate. The earth's crust was compressed and folded upwards. That created the Coast Ranges and the Transverse Ranges, which are composed of sea floor sediments.

The Coast Ranges, the largest of these mountain groups, are divided into northern and southern segments. The North Coast Ranges extend south from the Klamath River and the South Fork Mountains to San Francisco Bay. They are higher and broader than the South Coast Ranges. They draw more moisture from the air and are more heavily vegetated. The drier, less vegetated and more exposed South Coast Ranges, whose northernmost high peak is 3,849-foot Mt. Diablo east of San Francisco, extend southward to the Santa Ynez River in Santa Barbara County. There they merge into the Transverse Ranges.

The Transverse Ranges are unique. Every other major California mountain range trends north-south. Partly because of the San Andreas Fault, the Transverse Ranges break the pattern and trend east-west. They lie squeezed between the South Coast Ranges and the Peninsular Ranges. They create a natural barrier between Central and Southern California, as anyone who has climbed them on Interstate 5 north of Los Angeles knows. They extend west to form the Northern Channel Islands off Santa Barbara. They end 300 miles east, at the Mojave and Colorado deserts.

South of the Transverse Ranges, the Peninsular Ranges resume the north-south trend. They are characterized by small valleys, upland plains and rocky plateaus. Like the Transverse Ranges, the Peninsular Ranges are a popular place for motorized recreation.

The elevation change from sea to mountaintop along the coast is dramatic. The coastal mountains lack the Sierra Nevada's 14,000-foot peaks. But the transition from sea level to the tops of the coastal peaks and ridges — the relief — can seem as steep as the eastern escarpment of the Sierra along the Owens Valley. On the Big Sur Coast, the Santa Lucia Range vaults 5,000 feet above the surf. In the King Range, Kings Peak rises to 4,087 feet above sea level in less than three miles. The Transverse and Peninsular ranges both contain peaks that rise more than 10,000 feet. North of Fort Bragg, in Mendocino County in the North Coast Ranges, the the mountains' impenetrability forces Highway 1 to veer inland to terminate at U.S. 101, the Redwood Highway. Left isolated, this fragment of primitive coastline was nicknamed the Lost Coast, although Native Americans lived there for thousands of years and the past century has seen seamen, loggers, ranchers, even the oil industry and outlaw marijuana growers work the area. There are roads through the Lost Coast, but few are paved. This book will help you explore them so you can discover this still-wild bit of coastal California.

The vegetation in these geologic areas varies widely. There are wetlands and tinder-dry grasslands. There are redwoods and Douglas fir on the windward slopes of the Klamath and North Coast ranges. But go inland and the air is warmer and drier. One finds oaks, madrones, tanoaks and pines. Farther south, one finds more and more of those shrubby plants collectively called chaparral. The latter is especially prevalent in the Transverse and Peninsular ranges.

The range of wildlife is diverse. I'll long remember the morning in Six Rivers National Forest when a black bear strolled past my car, apparently unaware that I was watching it as I sipped coffee and listened to the news on the radio. Another time, along Low Divide Road in the same forest, I startled a bear in the road as I rounded a curve. There also are migrating gray whales, rare Roosevelt elk, mountain lions, harbor seals, sea lions, raptors, black-tailed deer, wild boars and rattlesnakes, to name only a few species. In December and January you can park on a promontory and watch gray whales migrating south from the rich feeding waters off Alaska to their warmer breeding waters off Baja California. Then, from March through early May, you can watch them swimming closer to shore as they head back toward Alaska with their calves. (The peak months are January and March.)

The climate is generally Mediterranean along the coast, with temperate wet winters and warm, dry summers. Storms typically approach from the north, and moisture there from rain and fog easily exceeds that in the south. Parts of the Lost Coast can receive as much as 200 inches of precipitation in a year, making the region one of the wettest in the United States. Crescent City averages 70 inches of rain annually. But semi-arid conditions exist in the Transverse and Peninsular ranges of Southern California. San Diego, at the western edge of the Peninsular Ranges, averages only 12 inches of rain a year.

While the western slopes of the mountains are dampened by rain and fog, you can have a near-desert experience farther inland in Quatal Canyon, in Ventura County. A few miles beyond Quatal Canyon you can walk among tall Jeffrey pines on San Emigdio Mountain. While the ocean side of the coastal mountains can be quite pleasant in summer, cross a single high ridge and you will find valleys that are hot, dry and buggy. In Los Padres National Forest, which encompasses about 1.95 million acres, mean annual rainfall varies from more than 60 inches at high elevations along the Monterey District coast to less than eight inches in some arid inland areas. Spring, when the grass is green and wildflowers are blooming, and fall generally are the best times to tour the coastal mountains.

Sometimes winter storms seriously damage rudimentary dirt roads like those in this book. Funding for maintaining and repairing these roads is limited and unlikely to increase, underscoring the need to check ahead and to go prepared.

These 50 drives will enable you to experience and, I hope, enjoy the variety offered by the coastal mountains, from those by the sea to those farther inland. I've tried to stay as close to the ocean as possible, but these mountains are broad, and urban centers inevitably force one inland. (Only about 42 percent of the shoreline is publicly owned and accessible.) By no means are these all the fine backroads that exist along the coast. Consider them instead your introduction to adventure driving in the region. You will find more on your own. Wherever you go you will find these mountains to be a beautiful and diverse resource for all to enjoy.

Touring backcountry byways

Driving along the California coast has been a favorite pastime for residents and visitors alike for decades, and for good reason. The beauty is astounding. But as appealing as paved coastal routes are, even more adventure and beauty lie waiting along the network of unpaved byways through the rugged coastal mountains between the Oregon border and Mexico. Some of these adventure roads, like those in the Lost Coast in Northern California, are quite remote and take you close to the ocean. Others, like the utterly spectacular Rincon to Shortcut route that begins in San Gabriel Canyon near Pasadena, are farther inland and surprisingly close to urban areas. Still others are convenient detours from heavily trafficked highways like Highway 1, U.S. 101, even Interstate 5.

Touring these backroads is a unique experience that can be done safely and responsibly. But you must take the necessary precautions and use good judgment to avoid injury to yourself and your passengers, and damage to the environment and your vehicle.

Here are some tips that will help you have a safe and rewarding experience:

KNOW WHERE YOU'RE GOING. The maps in this book are not intended for navigation. They are only at-a-glance maps to give you a general idea of where the drives are. For greater detail and navigational purposes, I generally recommend U.S. Forest Service maps. They're good, inexpensive general-purpose maps. They provide interesting background and important information, including rules and regulations, about their respective lands. They outline wilderness areas, where mechanized travel is prohibited, and identify both public and private lands. That will help you avoid trespassing. Some, however, are out of date. They can be purchased at national forest offices and information centers, or ordered from the Forest Service. (Addresses and telephone numbers are listed in the back of the book.) Many outdoor equipment and travel stores carry Forest Service maps as well as U.S. Geological Survey topographic maps. The latter show elevations and more detail, but you might have to buy more than one for each trip, so they can become expensive. They really aren't necessary for the drives in this book, however. Maps produced by the California State Automobile Association (CSAA) and the Automobile Club of Southern California (ACSC) are particularly good for this purpose. They are free to members. ACSC's maps are available to non-members at various retail outlets. You'll find many other good maps as well. Shop around.

Whichever maps you choose, study them before you leave. Learn your route before you start out. Bring the maps with you. Keep close track of where you've been along the way, and be aware of what's to come.

BE CAREFUL. The best advice is to not travel alone. There's no security like more than one vehicle. But the reality is that when you're on vacation, or off for a day or weekend, you'll probably have little choice but to go alone.

I believe that backcountry travel can be done safely alone, with proper precautions, preparation and due recognition of the potential hazards. But you still must recognize that there are risks in driving backcountry roads, just as there are risks in hiking backcountry trails. In particular, you must use good judgment whenever venturing onto beach sand, where you could get stuck. Many of the roads in this book are about as safe and easy as unpaved public roads can be. Some are much more rudimentary. Some are quite popular, so you might have company. The important thing to remember is that the condition of these roads can, and does, change. That's especially true during bad weather. You should call the appropriate authority before setting out to be sure your route is driveable.

Consider the time of day before you set out. Is it getting late? Don't get caught out there at night.

The best time to visit the coastal mountains is generally in the spring and fall. The coastline itself may be cool and comfortable in summer, but drive just a few miles inland and it can be unpleasantly hot and dry. As most Californians know, winter can bring tremendous, unrelenting downpours, turning backcountry roads into mud bogs blocked by slides and washouts. Many of these roads are therefore closed in winter.

Always be prepared to spend a few days out there, in case you get stuck or lost, or your vehicle breaks down. Carry adequate survival supplies, including water, for the number of people you have along.

Don't be tempted by excessively steep, rocky or sandy stretches. Know your vehicle. Don't overestimate what it can do. Many 4x4 owners will admit that they never got stuck so often or so badly before they bought a vehicle they thought could go anywhere. Always remember that help can be a long way off. Wear your seat belt. Have children in proper safety restraints. Always check the weather forecast before setting out, and watch for changes.

FOLLOW THE RULES. There are some, written and unwritten, even in places where it's likely no one will be looking. The intent behind them is to keep you safe. They also help to preserve these places from abusive and destructive activities that disturb wildlife, interfere with other lawful uses like livestock grazing, or damage the roads, the environment or archaeological and historic sites. Misconduct and mistakes can result in personal injury, damage to your vehicle, areas being closed, and possible legal penalties.

• Your vehicle must be fully street legal to take these drives. Obey all traffic laws.

• Never drive in designated wilderness areas, which are usually marked. Mechanized travel, including on motorcycles and mountain bikes, is not allowed in wilderness areas unless a legal route for such travel has been designated. You must always remain on established routes designated for motor vehicle use. Never make a new trail, or follow in the tracks of some irresponsible person who did.

• Obey regulatory and private property signs.

• Do not disturb archaeological or historic artifacts and sites. They are protected by federal and state laws. Some, like mines, may be on private land. View them from a distance. Do not use archaeological or historic sites for picnics or camping unless they are designated for those activities. The more time people spend at these sites, the greater the likelihood of damage. Learn the rules for camping in your chosen area, whether it's in a national park or national forest. Be sure to obtain a fire permit, available at any ranger station.

• Leave someone with a copy of your map showing the routes you plan to take. Let the person know when you'll return, and whom to call if you don't. Be sure to check in with that person when you return. Invite a friend to come along in his or her vehicle if you can.

• Camp only in established campsites, whether developed or primitive. If you are camping outside a developed site, camp on more resilient mineralized soil rather than soft grassy areas. Camp at least 100 feet from the banks of streams, ponds and lakes to avoid damage and pollution.

• Don't disturb wildlife or livestock. Leave gates as you find them.

• Leave no trace of your visit. Take out only what you bring in. Clean up after yourself and those who came before you. Haul out your trash.

• Be extremely careful around old mining operations. They're very dangerous, especially for children. View them from a distance. Never enter shafts, tunnels or holes.

• Avoid parking on grass; hot exhaust systems can ignite fires. Avoid steep hillsides, stream banks and meadows.

• If you get stuck or lost, stay with your vehicle unless you're certain that help is nearby. Your vehicle will be easier to find than you will be if you're walking through the mountains. It will provide shelter, too.

• Don't drive dirt roads in wet weather. Doing so can cause severe rutting. It can be dangerous, too. Also, mud that collects underneath your vehicle can transport organisms, like the root disease that devastates Port Orford cedars, to distant regions.

• Remember that the miners, loggers and settlers who carved roads through the mountains, forests and deserts of the West over the last century didn't have your safety in mind. Spurs from the main roads can be very rough. If the going does get real rough, ask yourself if it's worth the risk to you, your passengers and your vehicle.

If you are particularly interested in preserving the privilege of exploring backcountry byways, you might join Tread Lightly!, Inc., an organization founded to promote environmentally responsible use of off-highway vehicles. It is based in Ogden, Utah. Call 1-800-966-9900. Ask for their fine booklet, *The Tread Lightly! Guide to Responsible Four-Wheeling*.

BE PREPARED. Here's a basic checklist of some things to bring. (Develop your own if you wish.)

❑ Food and drinks. Remember that interior coastal valleys and mountains can be hot and dry in summer. Many, perhaps most, backcountry campgrounds no longer have water because of the high cost of meeting new federal drinking water standards. So if you plan to camp, bring plenty for drinking, cooking and washing.

❑ Always start with a full fuel tank; carry several gallons of extra fuel in a full, well-sealed container.

❑ A good first aid kit, with plenty of ointment and bandages for the inevitable scraped knees and elbows.

❑ Very good tires, a good spare and jack, tire sealant, air pump, pressure gauge, and a small board to support the jack on dirt. If you'll be driving on sand, you should bring two sturdy boards to use for traction in case you become stuck.

❑ Supplies, like sleeping bags and warm clothing, for spending the night in case you must.

❑ In case you run into trouble, bring some basic tools, including jumper cables, duct tape, electrical tape, baling wire, spare fuses, multipurpose knife, high-strength tow strap, fire extinguisher, shovel and a plastic sheet to put on the ground. An assortment of screws, washers, nuts, hose clamps and such could come in handy, too.

❑ Maps, compass
❑ Extra eyeglasses and keys
❑ Camera (still or video), film or video tape, tripod, binoculars
❑ Trash bags
❑ Flashlight or head lamp, extra batteries
❑ Matches and firewood
❑ Roadside emergency reflectors, flares, windshield scraper
❑ Altimeter, just for fun
❑ Watch
❑ Hats and clothing suitable for possible adverse weather
❑ Sunscreen and insect repellent
❑ Toilet paper (many backcountry campgrounds no longer provide it), paper towels, wet wipes.

I keep much of this stuff ready to go in a large plastic storage container. I'm often out alone scouting new drives, so sometimes I bring my mountain bike in case I get into a bind. I also use it to scout places that might damage my vehicle. If you do a lot of backcountry touring, think about getting a CB radio, even though their usefulness is limited. These days a cellular telephone might be handy, too.

I also have some tips on what to wear.

Forget shorts. Why would anyone expose his or her legs to brush, rocks, bugs, drying air and burning sun? Long pants and a shirt with breast pockets and sleeves you can roll up or down as needed are best, I've found. I also recommend high-topped leather boots with lug soles. If you are like me, you are going to do a lot of scrambling around to get that perfect camera angle. Ankle-high boots or shoes let debris in.

LEARN THE NECESSARY SKILLS. There are some driving techniques that can help you get where you're going and back again safely. They can also help you avoid damaging the roads you use and the places you visit.

• Try not to spin your tires, which digs up the earth and could get you stuck.

• Learn how to work your four-wheel-drive system before setting out. Think ahead as you drive; engage 4wd before you actually need it. When in doubt, scout ahead. Walk uncertain stretches of a route before you drive them.

• Occasionally you'll find that your low-range gears will provide both greater control and the high engine revs you need at slow speeds. I use mine a lot. Use them to climb or descend steep hills and to inch through tight spots without stalling. Avoid traversing steep hillsides if you can. Even if the road goes that way, stop if you're not confident it's safe. Don't try to turn around on a steep hillside. Back out. When climbing a steep hill, or going through mud, snow or sand, don't stop midway. Doing so could mean lost traction and stalling. Momentum can be everything, so keep moving. If you do stall going up a hill and must get out of the vehicle, put it in low-range first gear or reverse, and set the parking brake. Solidly block the wheels. When you try to get going again, play the parking brake against the clutch so you don't roll backwards. If you must back down a steep hill, put your vehicle in low-range reverse for greater control. Also use low-range to ease yourself down loose terrain. If your engine bogs down often in high range, switch to low range.

Remember that vehicles driving uphill have the right of way, if practical, because it's usually easier and safer for the vehicle going downhill to back up the hill.

• Have someone guide you through difficult spots. If the road has deep ruts, straddle them, letting them pass beneath the vehicle while the wheels ride high on the sides. Check your vehicle's clearance before driving over obstacles. Don't let rocks and such hit the big round parts, sometimes called "pumpkins," of your front and rear axles. Cracking or punching a hole in one will let vital oil drain out and expose the gears to dust and dirt. Run a tire over the obstacle if it's not too large, rather than letting it pass beneath your vehicle. Cross obstacles at an angle, rather than head-on.

• Avoid crossing streams if you can so you don't stir up the streambed. If you must cross a stream, do so only at an established crossing. Inspect streams before crossing. I pack a stick for checking the depth, comparing the depth to my vehicle. Cross slowly. Do not attempt to cross a road or streambed during a flood. Many busy stream crossings in Southern California's national forests have been paved with concrete. Such crossings can become slick with slime, so be careful.

• If you must cross soft material such as sand, maintaining momentum and speed is very important. To increase tire floatation on sand, lower tire pressure to 15 pounds or so. However, if a service station is far off, you will need either a hand pump or a small electric air compressor, like those available at department stores, to get your tires back up to proper inflation when you return to pavement.

• If you get stuck, calmly analyze the situation. With thought and work, you'll probably get out. Don't spin your tires if you get bogged down. That will dig you in deeper. Try this: Jack up the vehicle and backfill the hole beneath the stuck tire, building a base high enough to help you get a rolling start. If you're in sand, dampen it with water to firm it up. Lower the vehicle and remove the jack. If you get high-centered, meaning your undercarriage is lodged on something high and your tires have daylight between them and the ground, take out your jack and the little board you brought to set it on. Carefully jack up the vehicle, little by little, placing rocks, dirt and other materials under each suspended tire to build a higher base for it to rest on.

• If you reach a point where there are several routes to choose from and none has a sign, follow what appears to be the most heavily used route.

• When going through rocks or rutted stretches, keep your hands loose on the steering wheel, at 10 and 2 o'clock. Keep your thumbs on top of the wheel. If a front tire hits a rock or rut, the steering wheel could suddenly be jerked in an unexpected direction, possibly injuring a thumb with a steering wheel spoke.

MAINTAIN YOUR VEHICLE. Modern sport-utility vehicles are built to take families places that sedans, vans and station wagons either cannot go, or shouldn't. Despite their comforts, they are rugged transport. Equipped with four-wheel drive, protective steel skid plates, high ground clearance and all-terrain tires, they can go from the showroom straight into the hills without modifications. But backcountry roads can give even the toughest SUV quite a workout. So you've got to give your SUV more attention than you might be accustomed to giving a car. Start with your owner's manual. (It's in the glove compartment, right?) You might see two maintenance categories designed for two basic driving conditions: severe, and everything else. Anyone who uses this book falls into the severe category, and must do more maintenance. For example:

• Changing oil is a remarkably cheap and effective way to prolong engine life. Change it no later than every 3,000 miles, or sooner if you drive particularly dusty roads.

• Instead of getting a lube job at 15,000 miles, get one no later than every 7,500 miles, or immediately after returning from a dusty drive.

• Inspect your air filter at least every 3,000 miles. It's cheap and easy to clean or replace.

• Don't neglect gearbox oils, wheel bearing grease, brake and power steering fluids and coolant. Follow your owner's manual.

• Check the tires often. No part of your SUV will take a greater beating than they will. Inspect them, including your spare, closely before, during and after your drive. Do not rely on all-season highway tires. Along with heavy-duty shock absorbers designed for off-highway use, I recommend all-terrain tires. If you pass through an old mining area, you may get a nail in one or more tires. If you do, don't pull it out. Doing so will let the air out. Leave it alone, and get it repaired as soon as possible.

• When you get home, head for the car wash, especially if you've been on a beach. Thoroughly clean the vehicle. Put extra effort into the undercarriage, particularly the wheel wells.

READ. You'll enjoy your coastal adventures much more if you know something about the geology, flora, fauna and history of the region. Bookstores, visitor centers and other places have many fine titles to choose from. This book is not intended to be an exhaustive guide to exploring the coastal mountains. The "References & Suggested Reading" section in the back of the book lists some good books that have helped me understand, explore and write about the coast.

HAVE FUN! You can easily justify the expense of a sport-utility vehicle, especially in a state with so much beautiful public land. And as you travel the backcountry, tell me what you've found, whether it's mistakes in the book or additional trips and tips you'd like to see added in future editions. Write to me in care of the Post Register, P.O. Box 1800, Idaho Falls, ID, 83403.

Making it fun for all

Trying to keep kids, especially teenagers, happy on car trips has always been tough. But there are many things you can do to make touring the backcountry as fun and interesting for them as it is for you.

Probably the best advice I can give is this: Don't just drive. Stop, and stop often.

Watch for wildlife. Stop at beaches. And check out historical sites, like the abandoned lighthouse at Punta Gorda.

Smell the wildflowers. Study the different types of rocks and trees. There's nothing like running your hand over the bark of a giant coast redwood that is centuries old, or across a boulder of ancient seabed sediments. Get some good books on identifying wildflowers, birds, insects, rocks, vegetation and animals in the region. Get books on the geology and history of the area as well. They're available at local bookstores and visitor centers.

Make a photocopy of the area on the map where you'll be going. Get each child an inexpensive compass. Let them help you navigate and identify peaks, creeks, mine sites and other landmarks.

Let each child pack his or her favorite books and toys, but don't cram the car with stuff. Don't forget the sunscreen.

Bring at least one personal cassette player. Before leaving, go to your local public library and check out some children's cassette tapes. Better yet, buy some. You'll make good use of them for years to come.

Books on tape, something I listen to myself on long highway drives, are great diversions for children, too. Many video rental stores carry them.

Other items that have bought us quiet and good humor in the back seat are an inexpensive point-and-shoot camera the kids can use, and inexpensive binoculars. Now and then my son likes to have a notebook and pencil so he can pretend he's taking notes about our journeys just like dad.

If you have a responsible, licensed teenage driver on board, let him or her drive now and then. The sooner a teen learns backcountry driving skills, the longer he or she will remain an eager participant. Someday you may need an experienced co-pilot.

Of course, you must bring snacks, preferably the nutritious, non-sticky kind, and refreshing drinks. Milk products spoil quickly in heat and sunlight. Be sure cups have secure tops that you can poke straws through. Plastic garbage bags, paper towels, changes of clothing and wet wipes are good to have along, too.

Safety is always a concern because many hazards exist. Coastal waters can be treacherous. The beaches along the North Coast are beautiful, but the water is very cold and in many places the surf is too dangerous for swimming. You won't see lifeguards at remote beaches, either, so save swimming for designated places. When letting the kids play near the surf, watch the waves and the tide. Even on calm days, huge waves can crash ashore unexpectedly. Inland, the fire hazard can be very high. Never let children wander around old buildings, or get close to old mines. The latter are especially dangerous, and in many cases are private property.

Whether you travel with children or not, don't make the drive everything. Make it part of a day that draws on the huge range of experiences California's coastal mountains have to offer.

Author's favorites

This is the most subjective section of the book. The qualities that make a backcountry route appealing — scenery, solitude, the sense of adventure — are included in all 50 drives in varying proportions. I am uneasy saying one is better than another because we all have our individual preferences. I am partial to high-elevation vistas. And I like variety. Dense forests can be enchanting, but so can the woodlands of interior valleys. Narrow mountainside routes high above steep canyons are exhilarating, but so are windy bluffs overlooking the Pacific's pounding surf.

With that in mind, here are five of my favorite routes in California's coastal mountains:

Usal Road: Enchanting is really the best word I can use to describe this serpentine road through the remote, rugged and forested Lost Coast. When you're done, there are civilized amenities waiting at either end.

Punta Gorda: This windy point juts westward almost as far as Cape Mendocino to the north, the westernmost point in California. The view of gray-sand beaches, blue sky, the ocean and the steep mountains that leap from it is truly breathtaking. There's an abandoned lighthouse to visit as well.

Liebre Mountain: It's quite a ways inland, but it remains a fun and highly scenic route in the San Gabriel Mountains, one of the Transverse Ranges that shape the coast. Blockbuster vistas, and access is easy from Interstate 5.

Rincon to Shortcut: When you leave often-crowded San Gabriel Canyon and make the thrilling ascent to a long ridge, you will be amazed that one of California's best adventure backroads lies at the edge of the state's most urbanized area, the Los Angeles Basin.

Black Canyon Road: A spectacular route along a narrow, winding canyonside road in San Diego County north of Ramona. Great views, although they can be obscured by smog.

THE
DRIVES

Freshwater Lagoon Spit *(trip 4)*

Freshwater Lagoon Spit *(trip 4)*

Low Divide Road

LOCATION: Calif./Ore. border in Del Norte County; Smith River National Recreation Area in Six Rivers National Forest.

HIGHLIGHTS: This is the most northerly, and remote, route I describe. Lush forests, vistas, rugged scenery and varying road quality. Watch for bears. The Smith River, a protected wild and scenic waterway, is the state's only undammed river.

DIFFICULTY: Easy; a moderate moment or two.

TIME & DISTANCE: 5 hours; 50 miles.

GETTING THERE: I recommend starting at Crescent City. Take Elk Valley Road for a mile; turn right (east) onto Howland Road. It becomes a magnificent little dirt road through Jedediah Smith Redwood State Park. At U.S. 199 go east 4.5 miles; turn (left) north onto road 17N49.

THE DRIVE: Climb on 17N49 through forest. By mile 4 there are vistas westward toward the ocean, and later of interior ranges and deep valleys. At mile 7.6 turn right (east) onto Low Divide Road, a.k.a. Wimer Road (county road 305). At mile 9 is an incredible view down into the deep canyon of the North Fork of the Smith River. At 19.7 miles cross the river on a bridge, near a house known as Major Moore's (I couldn't learn why). The road becomes narrower and rougher. Soon you will drive along a ridge with more views. At about mile 25 cross a saddle, where you will see the McGrew 4x4 trail branching off to the left (north). From here the road becomes rocky as you creep along a narrow ledge. The forest will become lusher, with beautiful ferns. At about mile 30 there's a streamside place to rest. At 31.5 gated road 18N09 branches south to High Plateau. It's closed in the rainy season. (Muddy vehicles can spread a fungal root disease that is lethal to the region's rare and valuable Port Orford cedars.) In dry weather a Forest Service permit is required. It has some rough spots, and the brush can really do a job on your vehicle's paint. But it does go to a beautiful plateau with a unique botanical area. A few miles beyond this turnoff is an intersection. Left goes to a wilderness trailhead; go right. In 1.8 miles Holiday Mine Road, county road 315, goes south. It's a wonderful backcountry road that goes to U.S. 199 in 13.5 miles. Near the end you can detour southwest onto the Old Gasquet Toll Road, county road 314 *(trip 2)*.

REST STOPS: Camping, fishing, swimming in the Middle Fork of the Smith River. Food at Patrick Creek Lodge is great.

GETTING HOME: U.S. 199 west to U.S. 101 or northeast to Interstate 5 at Grants Pass, Ore.

MAPS: Six Rivers N.F.; CSAA, *Northern California Section.*

INFORMATION: Smith River National Recreation Area.

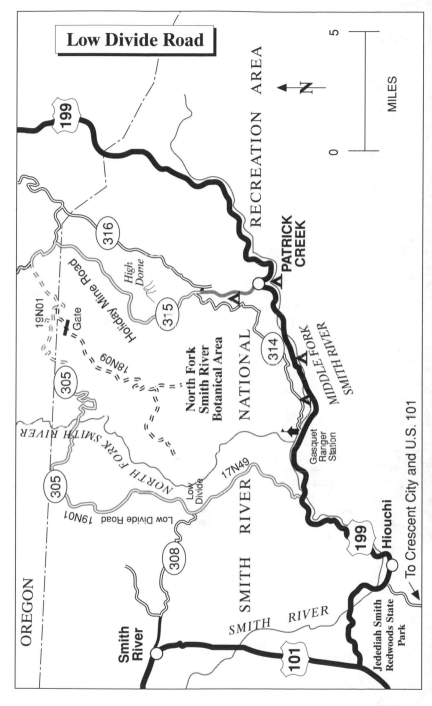

Low Divide Road

Old Gasquet Toll Road

LOCATION: Smith River National Recreation Area; Six Rivers National Forest; Del Norte County.

HIGHLIGHTS: Historic road, now county road 314, that was the predecessor to today's U.S. 199. Provides vistas, interpretive stops (including an old grave), and a great place to eat at the end. Look in boggy areas about midway along the route for insectivorous California pitcher plants, which lure insects with a fragrant nectar. Don't pick them; they could become a threatened or endangered species. Great wildflower displays, particularly azaleas, in spring.

DIFFICULTY: Easy gravel road.

TIME & DISTANCE: An hour; 17 miles.

GETTING THERE: This roughly east-west road north of U.S. 199 (the Smith River Scenic Byway) can be taken in either direction. In the town of Gasquet, turn right onto Middle Fork Gasquet Road, near the post office. Go about 0.1 mile to a fork and veer right. Go another 0.5 mile to a sign marked "Old Gasquet Toll Road." Turn right again and you're on your way. Set your odometer at 0. From Patrick Creek, go north on Patrick's Creek Road for about 3.5 miles. Cross a bridge, and veer left. That's it.

THE DRIVE: This is one of Smith River NRA's "Backroads Discovery Tours." It's an easy side trip off U.S. 199. Frenchman Horace Gasquet, who in 1857 founded the hamlet that bears his name, established the toll road in 1887 to link Crescent City to Waldo, Ore. It wasn't cheap for the times: a person on foot was charged 25 cents, a man and horse $1 and a one-horse vehicle $2.75. About 5 miles from Gasquet is Danger Point, where stagecoaches found it dangerous to pass. In another 3.1 miles is the grave of a guy named George Melderson. In 1900 he died at the Elk Horn Mine, near Patrick Creek Lodge. A friend buried him here.

REST STOPS: Let the kids out to play when you reach Patrick Creek. You'll see many fine primitive camp sites along Patrick Creek Road. Patrick Creek Lodge & Historical Inn is an excellent place to eat.

GETTING HOME: U.S. 199 west to U.S. 101, or northeast to Interstate 5 at Grants Pass, Ore.

MAPS: Six Rivers N.F. Get the brochure *Smith River National Recreation Area Backroads Discovery* at NRA headquarters in Gasquet. It explains significant points along the way.

INFORMATION: Smith River National Recreation Area.

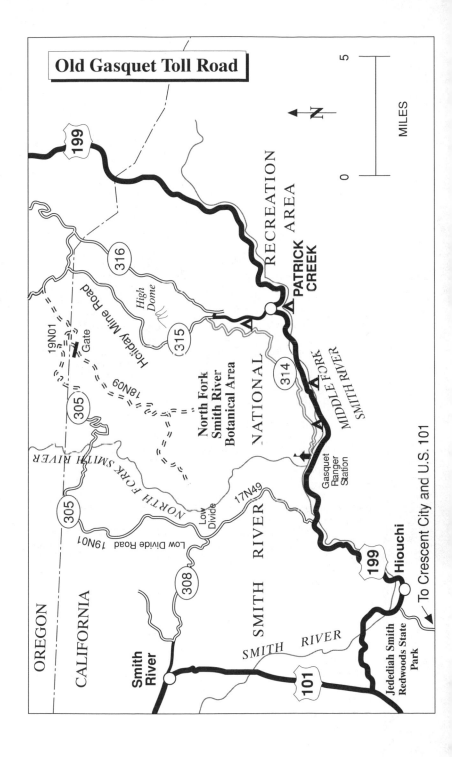

Old Gasquet Toll Road

Bear Harbor

LOCATION: This spur off Usal/Chemise Mountain roads *(trip 14)* is in the Lost Coast's 7,367-acre Sinkyone Wilderness State Park, in remote northwestern Mendocino County.

HIGHLIGHTS: Magnificent coastal scenery at a remote and historic site. Harbor seals, sea lions, migrating gray whales (best viewed in April & May, when they swim closer to shore as they head north with their calves). Nice beach. Open year-round.

DIFFICULTY: Road may be impassable when wet; in dry weather it's easy. There might be some rough spots south of Needle Rock.

TIME & DISTANCE: It's 3.4 miles from Four Corners to Needle Rock, and about 2.5 miles farther south to Bear Harbor.

GETTING THERE: At the Four Corners intersection 6.5 miles south of Shelter Cove Road, turn west onto Bear Harbor/Briceland Road (Mendocino County road 435). From U.S. 101 near Garberville, take Briceland Thorne Road/Shelter Cove Road west toward Shelter Cove. Turn left (south) on easy Chemise Mountain Road, and drive south to Four Corners.

THE DRIVE: The single-lane dirt road descends about 1,370 feet through forest of Douglas fir, tanoak and Pacific madrone to a grassy coastal terrace, site of the old settlement of Needle Rock that was named for an offshore rock. Sinkyone Indians hunted and fished in the area, until early settlers and federal troops hunted them nearly to extinction. Soon you'll see a barn, and small visitor center in a former ranch house built in the 1920s. In the late 1800s California's growing demand for lumber fueled North Coast logging. Lumber schooners sailed in and out of small and difficult "doghole" ports along the Mendocino and Humboldt coasts, such as Needle Rock, Bear Harbor and Usal. The ships hauled out various lumber products, including bark from tanoaks, which was used for the tannin needed by leather tanneries in San Francisco. To reach Bear Harbor, take the small road south from the visitor center, continuing beyond the point where county maintenance ends. 1.6 miles from the visitor center cross Flat Rock Creek, and in another 0.7 mile descend a steep and possibly rough section. Soon you'll reach road's end at a parking area and trailhead, at Orchard Camp. Backpackers can hike 16.7 miles of the Lost Coast Trail south to Usal. Or you can just follow the trail down to the beach at Bear Harbor, a 5-10-minute walk. In the late 1890s the Bear Harbor Lumber Co. built a 9-mile narrow-gauge railroad section down the Indian Creek drainage to move lumber to its wharf. Remnants of the tracks can be seen in the woods and on a bluff at the beach. In 1899 a seismic sea wave struck, destroying the Bear Harbor wharf and some of the railway, and drowning one man.

REST STOPS: 17 walk-in, tents-only fee campsites in the area. The only developed water source is at the Needle Rock Ranch House & Visitor Center, which also has picnic tables. The park no longer rents rooms in the ranch house. Gas up at Shelter Cove or Redway.

GETTING HOME: Take Briceland Thorne Road to U.S. 101 at Garberville, via Whitethorn. Or go north 6.5 miles to Shelter Cove Road, then east to U.S. 101.

MAPS: CSAA's *Northern California Section*; the park's brochure is very informative; the BLM's map for the KRNCA.

INFORMATION: Sinkyone Wilderness State Park.

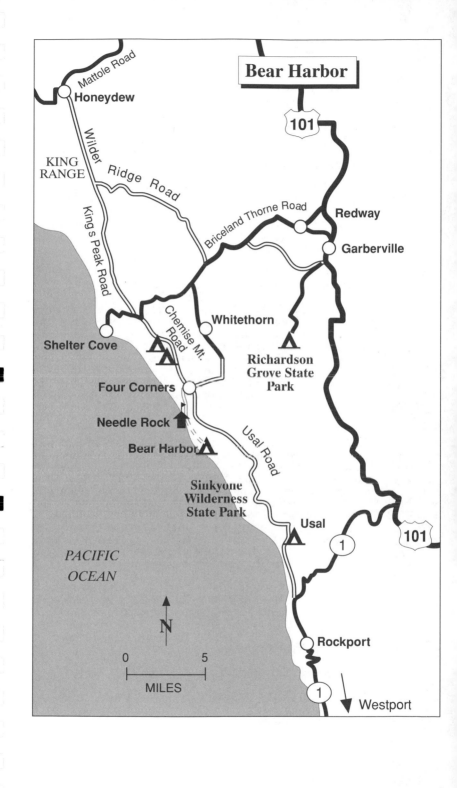

Bear Harbor

Freshwater Lagoon Spit

LOCATION: West of U.S. 101, Redwood National & State Parks, west of Orick.

HIGHLIGHTS: A chance to do some beach driving; camping on the spit (a small point of land extending into a body of water). Fishing. Driftwood collecting. The sunsets. You can make a loop if the mouth of Redwood Creek is passable.

DIFFICULTY: Easy to difficult; requires 4wd. People do get stuck now and then. You might air down your tires to 15 psi or so for better sand traction. (Air them back up when you're done.) Speed limit is 15 mph. Damp sand is generally firmer. The surf is dangerous. Obey the signs and drive only on the wave slope. Clean your vehicle afterwards.

TIME & DISTANCE: Almost 3 miles, depending on the tide. Take as much time as you want, but do watch the tide.

GETTING THERE: Access is a couple of miles west of Orick on U.S. 101. Look for the huge dirt parking area (dubbed "RV Alley" for obvious reasons) west of the highway. There are three posted beach access points for motor vehicles, which are not allowed on the dunes or vegetation. You can also access Orick Beach, at the mouth of Redwood Creek north of the information center, via Hufford Road. It goes west from the highway just north of the bridge over Redwood Creek. Half a mile past Gunst Road turn left off the paved road, at the sign for fishing access, then follow the creek to the beach.

THE DRIVE: The parking area is likely to be jammed with motorhomes, which can stay overnight. You will be sharing this beach with visitors who fish, or who just like to stroll along the beach or watch the sun set. Be careful and considerate. There are signs marking the limits of where you can drive. Many people drive on the damper and firmer sand on the wave slope. Motor vehicles are allowed on the beach from the south end of Freshwater Lagoon north about 3 miles, beyond the mouth of Redwood Creek to Mussel Point. You might not be able to cross Redwood Creek until mid or late summer. Check at the visitor center for rules and regulations.

REST STOPS: Lots of camping in the area. Ranger-led walks, evening programs, surf fishing and boating on Freshwater Lagoon, which is stocked with trout. The ocean is too cold and the surf is too dangerous for swimming.

GETTING HOME: U.S. 101.

MAP: Get the park brochure at the visitor center nearby.

INFORMATION: Redwood Information Center; Redwood National & State Parks.

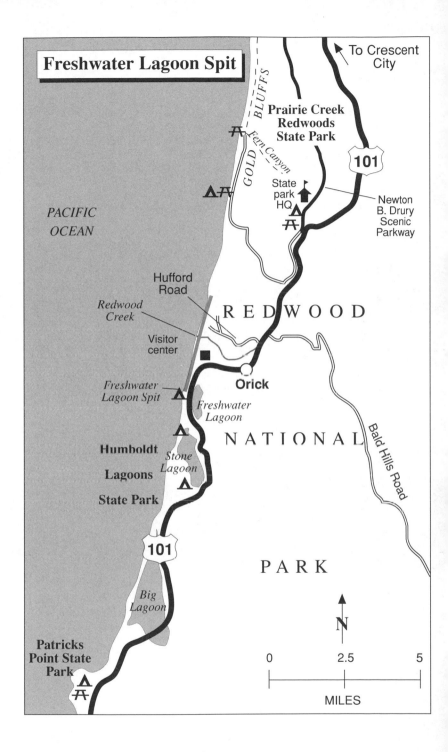

Freshwater Lagoon Spit

To Crescent City

Prairie Creek Redwoods State Park

GOLD BLUFFS

Fern Canyon

101

State park HQ

Newton B. Drury Scenic Parkway

PACIFIC OCEAN

Hufford Road

Redwood Creek

R E D W O O D

Visitor center

Freshwater Lagoon Spit

Orick

Freshwater Lagoon

Humboldt

Stone Lagoon

N A T I O N A L

Bald Hills Road

Lagoons

State Park

101

P A R K

Big Lagoon

N

Patricks Point State Park

0   2.5   5

MILES

Hoopa Valley Loop

LOCATION: Humboldt County, northeast of Eureka.

HIGHLIGHTS: Redwood National & State Parks; Tall Trees Trail, site of the world's tallest tree (you must get a free permit and combination to the locked gate from the Redwood Information Center west of Orick between 8 a.m. & 2 p.m.); Hoopa Valley Indian Reservation; the Klamath River (California's second largest) and the Trinity River.

DIFFICULTY: Easy on well-graded dirt and gravel roads.

TIME & DISTANCE: 3 hours and almost 70 miles, excluding the 11.8-mile (round-trip) drive and 2.6-mile (round-trip) hike to the tall trees (steep; no water or services).

GETTING THERE: You can start on Bald Hills Road north of Orick, on U.S. 101, and go southeast to come out on state Highway 299. If you prefer to go north (the way I describe the drive), from U.S. 101 north of Arcata take Highway 299 northeast about 18 miles. As you descend the east side of Lord Ellis Summit, go left (north) onto Bair Road. Reset your odometer.

THE DRIVE: The road is paved for the first 3.9 miles, then the road forks. Go right to Hoopa, about 17 miles farther on a gravel road through a shady forest. At 14 miles is a vista point overlooking Hoopa Valley and interior ranges. The road becomes asphalt at mile 18.5. At mile 20, near town, there's a park with a playground on the right. Drive through town, heading north along the Trinity River for almost 15 miles to the bridge over the Klamath River at Martin's Ferry. Cross the bridge onto Bald Hills Road. The good dirt and gravel road climbs through forest from about 430 feet elevation to over 3,000 feet. The views are great once you cross into the national park (a no-fee entrance here). If the gate is open to the lookout atop Schoolhouse Peak (el. 3,092), go on up for a fantastic vista across redwood forests, white oak woodlands and coastal grasslands. The road is paved 4.8 miles farther. The gate to the Tall Trees Trail is almost 11 miles from the lookout; U.S. 101 is 7 miles farther.

REST STOPS: The exotic hike through Fern Canyon in Prairie Creek Redwoods State Park is a must. The park includes rare Roosevelt elk, oceanside camping, picnicking and hiking. The entrance is 1.5 miles north of the Bald Hills Road turnoff on U.S. 101. Hoopa has all services.

GETTING HOME: U.S. 101 north or south.

MAP: CSAA, *Northern California Section.*

INFORMATION: Humboldt County; Redwood Information Center; Redwood National & State Parks.

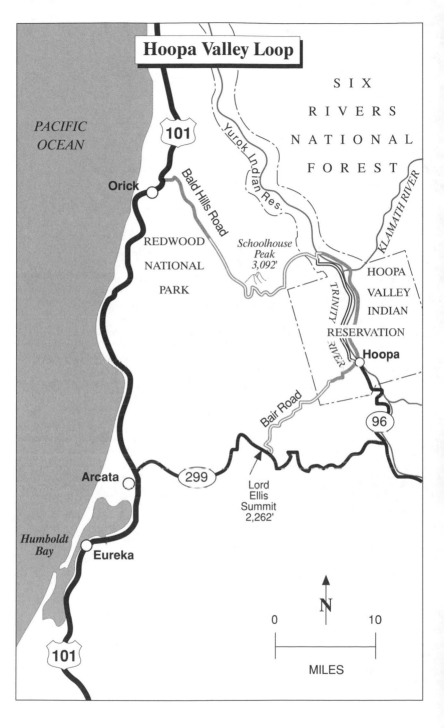

Hoopa Valley Loop

PACIFIC
OCEAN

SIX RIVERS NATIONAL FOREST

Yurok Indian Res.

KLAMATH RIVER

101

Orick

Bald Hills Road

Schoolhouse
Peak
3,092'

REDWOOD
NATIONAL
PARK

HOOPA
VALLEY
INDIAN
RESERVATION

TRINITY RIVER

Hoopa

Bair Road

96

Arcata

299

Lord
Ellis
Summit
2,262'

Humboldt
Bay

Eureka

101

N

0   10

MILES

Eel River Wildlife Area

LOCATION: South of Humboldt Bay, at the mouth of the Eel River.

HIGHLIGHTS: Eel River Delta's rich array of wildlife.

DIFFICULTY: Easy; some ruts and rough spots.

TIME & DISTANCE: 1.5 hours; 6.3 miles round-trip.

GETTING THERE: Take the Hookton Road/Loleta off-ramp from U.S. 101, south of Eureka. Cross Eel River Drive, go through a farm, across a one-lane bridge and into the hills. About 5 miles from Eel River Drive you will be on Table Bluff Road. Soon South Jetty Road veers right (north). There is an unofficial campground used by homeless people and transients, to the left, at the bend in the road. Drive through the camp-ground and there's a sign for the wildlife refuge. The road is straight ahead, going south. Set your odometer at 0.

THE DRIVE: It starts out on soft sand, but soon becomes firm as you pass a large marsh on the left. The ocean is beyond the rise to your right. You'll see lots of signs warning that off-road travel is prohibited. At mile 2 there's a place to pull off. A beach strewn with driftwood is a short walk over the rise, but the surf is dangerous. You will need a Fish & Game permit to collect driftwood. This delta is one of California's largest coastal wetlands, providing essential habitat for migratory birds using the Pacific Flyway, one of four major avian migra-tion routes in North America. (The California coast is at its western edge.) If birds are what you want to see, visit during the fall migration (Sept.-Oct.). But it will be cold and wet then. The delta's raptor population, one of the coast's largest, includes ospreys, red-tailed hawks, kestrels, endangered pere-grine falcons and occasionally eagles. It's a popular place for bird and whale watching (gray whales migrate off-shore December through early May). You'll reach the end of the spit at mile 3.2, where you may see seals and sea lions. This is a very pretty place, but unfortunately other visitors leave litter behind. Do the right thing; clean up after them.

REST STOPS: Have lunch at the end of the road.

GETTING HOME: Return to U.S. 101.

MAP: This road doesn't appear on any maps that I know of, except the one to the right. But any map that will get you from U.S. 101 to South Jetty Road at the mouth of Humboldt Bay will do.

INFORMATION: California Department of Fish & Game, Eureka.

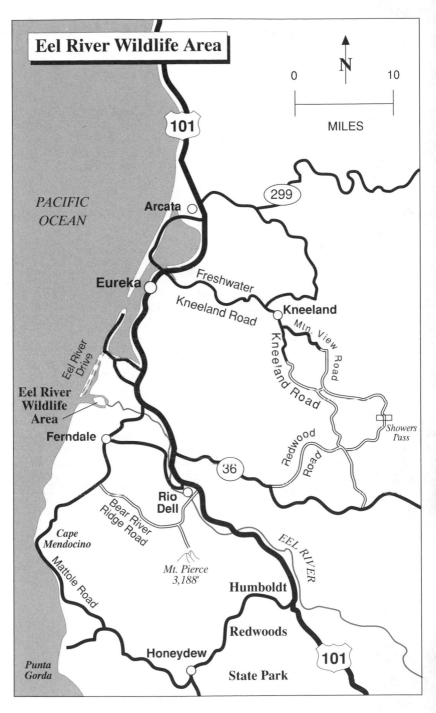

Eel River Wildlife Area

N

0   10

MILES

PACIFIC
OCEAN

101

Arcata

299

Eureka

Freshwater

Kneeland Road

Kneeland

Mtn. View Road

Kneeland Road

Eel River Drive

Eel River
Wildlife
Area

Showers
Pass

Ferndale

Redwood Road

36

Rio
Dell

Bear River
Ridge Road

Cape
Mendocino

Mattole Road

Mt. Pierce
3,188'

EEL RIVER

Humboldt

Redwoods

Honeydew

State Park

Punta
Gorda

101

Bear River Ridge Road

LOCATION: Humboldt County, southwest of Rio Dell.

HIGHLIGHTS: Spectacular coastal scenery from more than 2,700 feet above the ocean as you drive atop rolling hills overlooking Cape Mendocino, the westernmost point in California, and interior mountains and valleys. Nearby Ferndale, founded in 1852, is famous for its Eastlake- and Queen Anne-style Victorian homes.

DIFFICULTY: Couldn't be easier, or prettier.

TIME & DISTANCE: An hour; almost 10 miles, including 6.4 miles of hard-packed, well-maintained dirt.

GETTING THERE: I describe it going west from Rio Dell so you'll get the coastal view, exiting on Mattole Road south of Ferndale. In Rio Dell, a logging town, take Monument Road to Pacific. Keep left on Monument. Almost 5 miles from town go right (west) onto dirt Bear River Ridge Road. Monument continues to a locked gate below a fire lookout. If you're southbound on U.S. 101 and would like a scenic detour, take this drive eastward. To do so, take Mattole Road south from Ferndale for 6 miles. Turn left (southeast) onto Upper Bear Road, which reaches Bear River Ridge Road in 1.7 miles.

THE DRIVE: Climb and twist through trees and across undulating, grassy hilltops as clouds of fog break up overhead, casting moving shadows on the rolling hills. The view of the valley and mountains from the ridge is outstanding. The roadbed will be broken pavement as you approach Bear River Ridge Road, which is a picture-perfect one-lane dirt road atop a wind-swept crest. Watch for grazing cattle. After 6.4 miles Bear River Ridge Road becomes a paved, though idyllic, country lane that becomes Upper Bear Road 1.7 miles before reaching Mattole Road. Ferndale is 6 miles to your right (north). In 1859 the discovery of oil in the Bear River area led to an influx of settlers, but when oil extraction proved unprofitable many of the new arrivals left. The hamlet of Petrolia, to the south, is near the area on the North Fork of the Mattole River where California's first commercial oil well was drilled, in 1865.

REST STOPS: Ferndale; many places along the coast; pretty A.W. Way County Park (picnic tables, camping, playground, flush toilets, cold showers, river access, fishing) on the way to Honeydew, where you'll find a quaint country store and gas.

GETTING HOME: Magnificent Mattole Road, one of the most beautiful paved drives in America, will take you to U.S. 101 via Ferndale or Honeydew.

MAP: CSAA, *Northern California Section.*

INFORMATION: Humboldt County.

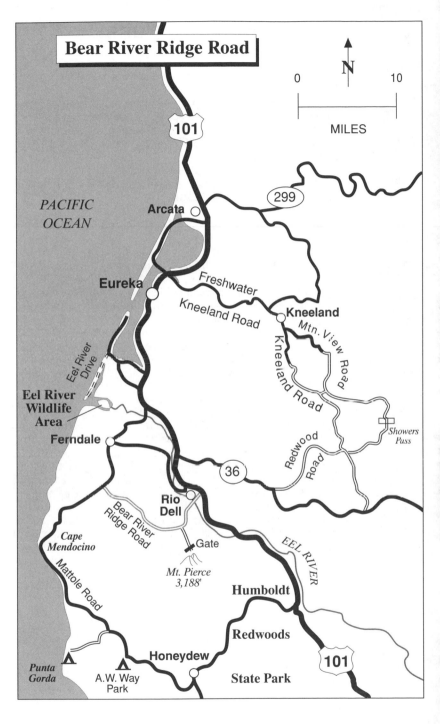

Bear River Ridge Road

N

0   10

MILES

PACIFIC
OCEAN

101

299

Arcata

Eureka

Freshwater

Kneeland Road

Kneeland

Mtn. View Road

Kneeland Road

Eel River
Drive

Eel River
Wildlife
Area

Ferndale

36

Redwood Road

Showers
Pass

Bear River
Ridge Road

Rio
Dell

Cape
Mendocino

Gate

EEL RIVER

Mt. Pierce
3,188'

Humboldt

Mattole Road

Redwoods

101

Punta
Gorda

A.W. Way
Park

Honeydew

State Park

Showers Pass

LOCATION: Humboldt County, southeast of Eureka.

HIGHLIGHTS: A narrow, pastoral dirt road through grassy hills dotted with wildflowers in spring; woodlands and valleys. Outstanding views to the west of mountains and banks of coastal fog, from well over 3,000 feet elevation. You will pass through logged areas, however.

DIFFICULTY: Easy; one steep spot where 4wd is helpful. Watch for logging trucks and cattle.

TIME & DISTANCE: 3.5 to 4 hours; about 42 miles from state Highway 36 to Kneeland.

GETTING THERE: I describe this loop going basically north to Eureka. At Alton on U.S. 101, south of Eureka, turn east on state Highway 36 toward Bridgeville. Go 11.4 miles, through Van Duzen Redwoods Park. Turn left (northeast) on Redwood House Road. Set your odometer at 0.

THE DRIVE: For the first 5 miles or so you will get a first-hand look at what clearcutting is. Take note of the large old redwood stumps. Follow the crude signs for road No. 645. After the clear-cut area you will enter hills with grassy pastures. Go through the opening in the fence at about mile 7.75. There is private land on either side of the road. Soon you will drive through a canyon on a one-lane dirt road, then enter pretty Yager Valley. Continue east, passing Kneeland Road on the left and, in another mile, its southerly branch on the right. If you don't care to complete the loop to Eureka, you can turn south here and exit onto Highway 36 at Bridgeville. To do the loop, stay on Showers Pass Road. In a few miles you'll descend into a canyon via switchbacks. I recommend using 4wd for the climb out so your rear tires don't spin and tear up the roadbed. When you reach Stapp Road, on the right, you're on Showers Pass, at about 3,300 feet. Look west; magnificent, isn't it? The dirt roadbed will be oiled as you descend into, and then climb out of, yet another beautiful valley. At about mile 30.5 go right onto Mountain View Road, which becomes paved. Continue to U.S. 101.

REST STOPS: Swimming, picnicking and playgrounds at Freshwater County Park (day use only), 9.5 miles northwest of Kneeland and 7 miles east of Eureka on Freshwater Road.

GETTING HOME: U.S. 101 north or south.

MAP: CSAA, *Northern California Section*.

INFORMATION: Humboldt County.

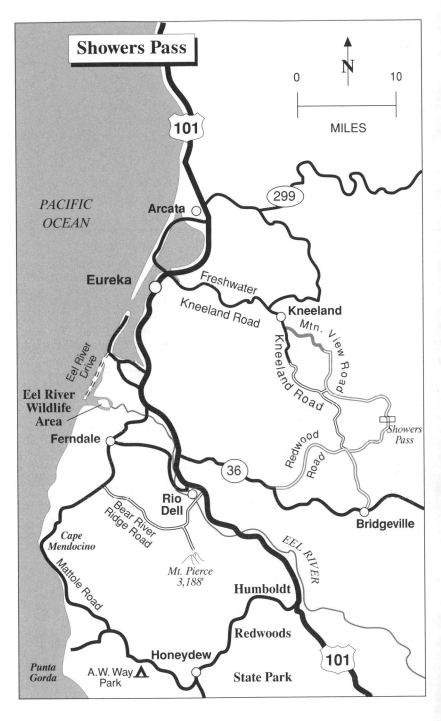

Showers Pass

N

0 — 10
MILES

PACIFIC OCEAN

101

299

Arcata

Eureka

Freshwater

Kneeland Road

Kneeland

Mtn. View Road

Kneeland Road

Eel River Drive

Eel River Wildlife Area

Ferndale

Redwood Road

Showers Pass

36

Bridgeville

Rio Dell

Bear River Ridge Road

Cape Mendocino

EEL RIVER

Mattole Road

Mt. Pierce 3,188'

Humboldt

Punta Gorda

A.W. Way Park

Honeydew

Redwoods

State Park

101

Punta Gorda

LOCATION: Lost Coast at the northern end of the King Range National Conservation Area, Humboldt County.

HIGHLIGHTS: A spectacular drive on some of the most primitive coastline in the nation. Abandoned Punta Gorda lighthouse; an old ranch. Sea lions, various birds, tide pools, spring whale-watching, fishing in the ocean or Mattole River.

DIFFICULTY: Easy when dry; may be impassable when wet. Windy Point Road closes November 1 for the rainy season.

TIME & DISTANCE: 2 hours; 7.2 miles round-trip.

GETTING THERE: South of Petrolia, take Lighthouse Road west for 4.9 miles from the bridge on Mattole Road over the Mattole River. Turn left onto Prosper Ridge Road.

THE DRIVE: After half a mile the view of the Mattole River estuary and the mountains vaulting from the sea is fantastic. By mile 2, after climbing switchbacks (where I shot the cover photo), pass through a forested area. At mile 2.3 take a two-track that branches right, through grassy hills. This is Windy Point Road. Go through the gate, traverse a hilltop, then drop steeply down a rutted track to the point. In Spanish the name of this rounded cape means Fat Point or Massive Point. It is a blustery place that protrudes into the Pacific almost as far as Cape Mendocino to the north, the westernmost point in California. This is earthquake country. The hamlet of Petrolia, 3 miles west of where California's first drilled commercial oil well was sunk in 1865, sits on the San Andreas Fault. North of Punta Gorda the fault curves out to sea, then splinters northward. Just off shore three plates of the earth's crust — the North American, Pacific and Gorda plates — collide at the so-called Mendocino Triple Junction. A 7.1 temblor in 1992 caused major damage to buildings in Petrolia and Ferndale.

REST STOPS: Mattole C.G., at the end of Lighthouse Rd., is windy and shadeless. I prefer A.W. Way County Park, 8 miles south toward Honeydew. From the Mattole River you can take a 3.2-mile (one-way) seaside hike south to the lighthouse. Or hike a mile south of Windy Pt. Near the lighthouse is the old Beatty cabin and other relics of ranching in the area. The lighthouse was built in 1911 after a number of shipwrecks. The *Columbia* sank in 1907, killing 87 people. Obsolete by the late 1940s, the Coast Guard abandoned the lighthouse in 1951. Near the trail are two old oil storage tanks. The hulk on the beach is an old buoy. Food and gas are available at Petrolia.

GETTING HOME: Scenic Mattole Road goes north to Ferndale, or south and east through Honeydew to U.S. 101.

MAP: U.S. Bureau of Land Management's *King Range National Conservation Area Recreation Guide.*

INFORMATION: U.S. Bureau of Land Management in Arcata. BLM's King Range headquarters.

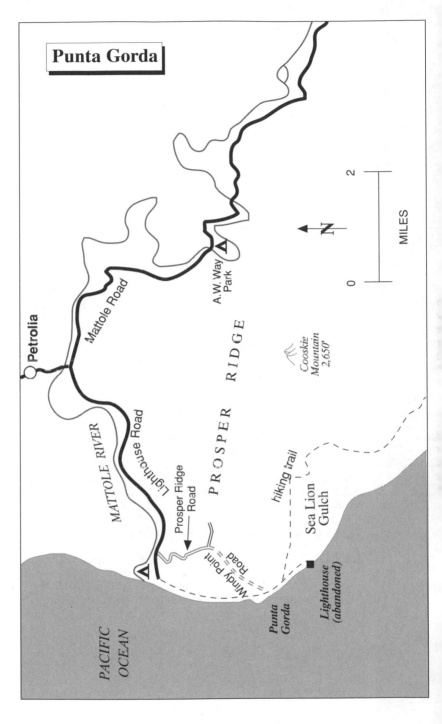

Punta Gorda

Petrolia

Mattole Road

MATTOLE RIVER

Lighthouse Road

Prosper Ridge Road

PROSPER RIDGE

Cooskie Mountain 2,650'

A.W. Way Park

hiking trail

Windy Point Road

Sea Lion Gulch

Punta Gorda

Lighthouse (abandoned)

PACIFIC OCEAN

N

MILES

0   2

Smith-Etter Road

LOCATION: Lost Coast (King Range National Conservation Area), south of Honeydew in Humboldt County.

HIGHLIGHTS: Views of the Mattole Valley and the rugged mountains.

DIFFICULTY: Easy. Closed Nov. 1-March 31.

TIME & DISTANCE: 1.75 hours; 19.7 miles round-trip.

GETTING THERE: From Honeydew, go south on the Wilder Ridge Road for 1.5 miles. There is a sign for the Smith-Etter Road on the right. Set your odometer at 0.

THE DRIVE: This road will take you through forest high into the King Range to Telegraph Ridge, beyond which the road is closed to motor vehicles by a gate. It climbs fairly steeply at first, from about 460 feet elevation to about 3,200 feet, providing a bird's-eye view of a Tolkienesque landscape of coastal mountains and the Mattole Valley. At 8.3 miles there's a good place to pull over to savor the vista of the ocean and coast. Soon you will reach the locked gate, where the mountains to the west form a narrow V through which you can see the ocean.

REST STOPS: Relax on the porch of the country store at charming little Honeydew, where annual rainfall averages more than 100 inches. (Nearby areas can get as much as 200 inches in a year.) It's a hike of about 3 miles (one-way) from where the road is closed, at about 2,300 feet above sea level, down to the ocean. Allow extra time for the steep slog back up. About 8.2 miles northwest of Honeydew on paved Mattole Road is lovely A.W. Way Memorial County Park. Wheel-chair accessible, it has picnic tables, a playground, Mattole River access, camping, flush toilets, cold showers and a public telephone.

GETTING HOME: It's 23 slow and serpentine miles on Mattole Road from Honeydew to U.S. 101 via Humboldt Redwoods State Park. Or take gorgeous Mattole Road from Honeydew north to Petrolia (3 miles west of where California's first commercial oil well was drilled, in 1865), Ferndale and U.S 101.

MAP: Bureau of Land Management's map for the *King Range National Conservation Area*.

INFORMATION: U.S. Bureau of Land Management in Arcata. BLM's King Range headquarters.

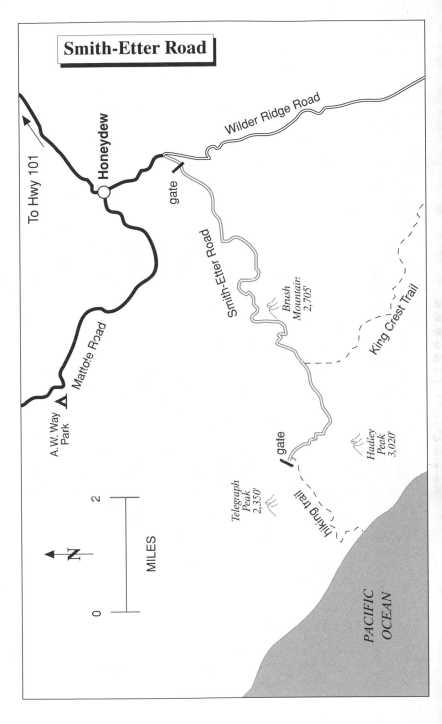

Smith-Etter Road

To Hwy 101

Honeydew

Wilder Ridge Road

gate

Smith-Etter Road

Brush Mountain 2,705'

King Crest Trail

Mattole Road

A.W. Way Park

gate

Hadley Peak 3,020'

Telegraph Peak 2,350'

hiking trail

N

MILES

0   2

PACIFIC OCEAN

Dyerville Loop Road

LOCATION: Humboldt County, northeast of Garberville.

HIGHLIGHTS: Magnificent vistas to the west that include the coastal King Range. Like the nearby Bell Springs Road, this, too, is an outstanding alternative to U.S. 101 that climbs to over 3,000 feet elevation.

DIFFICULTY: Easy; well-maintained dirt and gravel.

TIME & DISTANCE: 1.5 to 2 hours; about 37 miles from Garberville to U.S. 101.

GETTING THERE: You can take this in either direction. I describe it from Garberville north to Avenue of the Giants and U.S. 101. Take Redwood Drive north from town for 0.3 miles; turn right (east) onto paved Alderpoint Road. Drive about 7 miles, then turn left (north) onto Dyerville Loop Road. Set your odometer at 0.

THE DRIVE: You will quickly begin a long, serpentine climb up Mail Ridge, passing hills of golden grass, and madrone and evergreen trees. Depending on the weather, you may be able to see a thick blanket of fog on the ocean to the west, across the jumbled mass of rugged mountains along the Lost Coast. At about mile 11.5 you'll cross from the west side of the ridge to the east side, getting a grand view of interior mountains and valleys far to the east. There will be short stretches of pavement as you pass residences. By 21.7 miles the road becomes paved, and in another mile it passes Eel Rock Road, on the right. Continue to state Highway 254 and U.S. 101, or continue on Dyerville Loop Road where it branches northwest from Elk Creek Road toward the Eel River.

REST STOPS: Garberville; Humboldt Redwoods State Park. Drive Avenue of the Giants, a magnificent paved road through ancient redwoods.

GETTING HOME: U.S. 101 north or south.

MAP: CSAA, *Northern California Section.*

INFORMATION: Humboldt County.

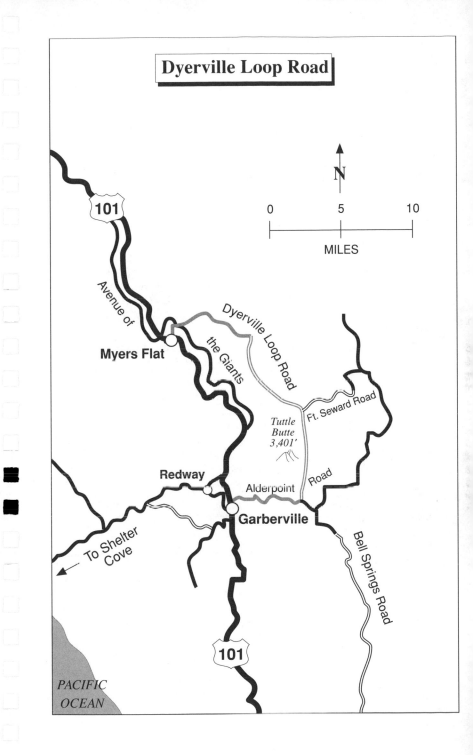

Dyerville Loop Road

Kings Peak Road

LOCATION: Lost Coast (King Range National Conservation Area), north of Shelter Cove in Humboldt County. This road is called Horse Mountain Road on some editions of the U.S. Bureau of Land Management's map of the KRNCA, and on CSAA's Northern California Section map.

HIGHLIGHTS: A beautiful, tortuous corridor through coastal forest of ferns, Douglas fir, tanoak and chemise, with alternating views of the ocean and inland areas.

DIFFICULTY: Easy in good weather.

TIME & DISTANCE: 17 miles; an hour.

GETTING THERE: From Redway, near Garberville (on U.S. 101), drive west 19 miles first on Briceland Thorne Road, then Shelter Cove Road; turn right (north) onto Kings Peak Road 4 miles before Shelter Cove. From Honeydew, on Mattole Road, take Wilder Ridge Road south for 7.7 miles (it becomes gravel after 2 miles). Kings Peak Road angles to the right, heading south (this is the way I go).

THE DRIVE: Almost directly to the west is this road's namesake and the highest point in the King Range, Kings Peak, which rises to 4,087 feet in less than 3 miles from the sea. Switchback down a series of hairpin turns. Cross the bridge over Bear Creek, then climb and snake your way through a bit of rain forest on a one-lane road. Notice the brooks gurgling down from the high, steep ridge. Be very careful as you approach the many blind curves; there might well be someone else coming in the opposite direction. On the right at mile 2.8 is the turnoff to King Range Road, which goes to beautiful Saddle Mountain Road *(trip 13)*. About 3 miles farther you will pass the Horse Mountain Recreation Site, where the southern end of Saddle Mountain Road joins Kings Peak Road. Farther south is a similar site, Tolkan. Paved Shelter Cove Road is 3.6 miles farther.

REST STOPS: Horse Mountain and Tolkan recreation sites along the way (camping & day use); at either end, the porch of quaint Honeydew Store and the town of Shelter Cove. Both have gas; the latter has camping, motels and restaurants, too.

GETTING HOME: Depending on where you end, go north to Honeydew and U.S. 101, or east to Redway and U.S. 101.

MAPS: BLM's map for the KRNCA; CSAA's *Northern California Section*.

INFORMATION: U.S. Bureau of Land Management in Arcata. BLM's King Range headquarters.

ALSO TRY: Paradise Ridge Road, north of Shelter Cove Road about 2 miles east of Chemise Mountain Road, goes 2.5 miles to the top of Queen's Peak (el. 2,800 ft.) for great vistas. It's a fine alternative to hiking up Kings Peak.

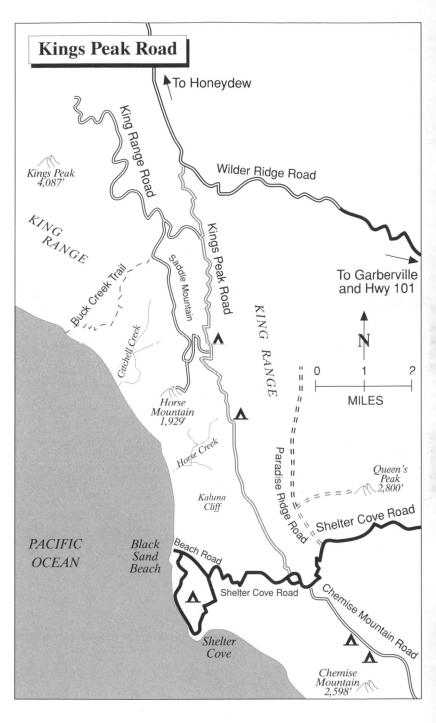

Kings Peak Road

To Honeydew

King Range Road

Kings Peak
4,087'

Wilder Ridge Road

KING
RANGE

Saddle Mountain

Buck Creek Trail

Gitchell Creek

Kings Peak Road

KING RANGE

To Garberville
and Hwy 101

N

0   1   2
MILES

Horse
Mountain
1,929'

Horse Creek

Paradise Ridge Road

Queen's
Peak
2,800'

Kaluna
Cliff

Shelter Cove Road

PACIFIC
OCEAN

Black
Sand
Beach

Beach Road

Shelter Cove Road

Chemise Mountain Road

Shelter
Cove

Chemise
Mountain
2,598'

Saddle Mountain Road

LOCATION: Lost Coast (King Range National Conservation Area), Humboldt County between Shelter Cove and Honeydew.

HIGHLIGHTS: Access via serpentine Kings Peak Road, called Horse Mountain Road on some Bureau of Land Management maps of the KRNCA. Tremendous vistas of the ocean from about 3,000 feet above sea level.

DIFFICULTY: Easy.

TIME & DISTANCE: An hour or less; 5.7 miles.

GETTING THERE: From Honeydew, take Wilder Ridge Road south to Kings Peak Road. Take Kings Peak Road south 2.8 miles, then turn right onto King Range Road. In 2 miles Saddle Mountain Road continues ahead, climbing toward a ridge. (King Range Road branches right to deadend in 4.5 miles at Lightning trailhead.) If you start at Shelter Cove, from Shelter Cove Road take Kings Peak Road north for 6.2 miles to Saddle Mountain Road, on your left. I start at Honeydew.

THE DRIVE: Reset your odometer upon turning off Kings Peak Road onto King Range Road. The road will climb steeply, so use 4wd to keep your rear tires from spinning on the loose rock and dirt roadbed. At mile 2 angle left onto Saddle Mountain Road, which climbs to Horse Mountain Ridge. By mile 4.2, as you zigzag along the crest of the ridge, the views of the ocean and inland areas are outstanding. At a sharp left bend in the road at mile 6, you will see on the right the narrow Horse Mountain spur. It is closed in 1.1 miles, and turning around is difficult. I recommend walking or riding a mountain bike. The views of the mountains rising from the ocean are great. Kings Peak Road is 1.2 miles beyond the Horse Mountain spur.

REST STOPS: Horse Mountain and Tolkan recreation sites along the way (camping & day use; Tolkan is wheel-chair accessible); at either end, the quaint Honeydew Store and the town of Shelter Cove. Both have gas. The latter has all services. Streamside tenting at Honeydew Creek Campground, a mile south of Honeydew on Wilder Ridge Road. If you like hiking on steep terrain, from Lightning trailhead you can climb about 2,000 feet in about 2.5 miles to reach the summit of 4,087-ft. Kings Peak, the highest in the King Range.

GETTING HOME: Depending on where you end, go north to Honeydew and U.S. 101, or east to Redway and U.S. 101.

MAP: BLM's map for the KRNCA. This road isn't on CSAA's *Northern California Section* map.

INFORMATION: U.S. Bureau of Land Management in Arcata. BLM's King Range headquarters.

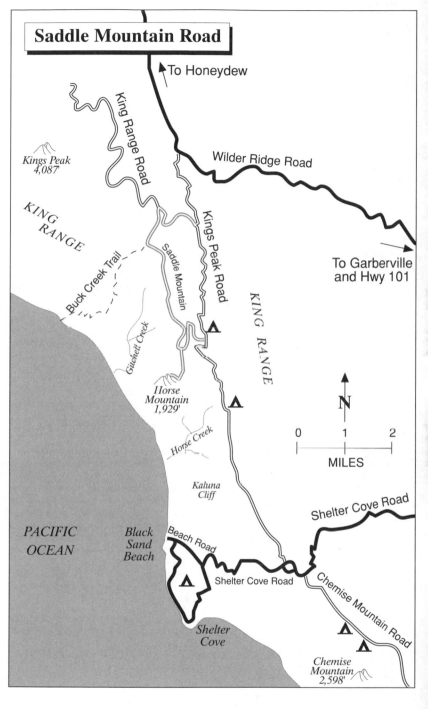

Saddle Mountain Road

To Honeydew

King Range Road

Wilder Ridge Road

Kings Peak
4,087'

KING
RANGE

Kings Peak Road

Buck Creek Trail

Saddle Mountain

Guthell Creek

KING RANGE

To Garberville
and Hwy 101

Horse
Mountain
1,929'

Horse Creek

N

0 1 2
MILES

Kaluna
Cliff

Shelter Cove Road

PACIFIC
OCEAN

Black
Sand
Beach

Beach Road

Shelter Cove Road

Chemise Mountain Road

Shelter
Cove

Chemise
Mountain
2,598'

Usal Road

LOCATION: Lost Coast, northwestern Mendocino County and southwestern Humboldt County. Crosses Sinkyone Wilderness State Park and the King Range National Conservation Area.

HIGHLIGHTS: Tortuous road, much of it along high ridges, through enchanting forest of second-growth redwood and Douglas fir, madrone, tanoak and ferns; the King Range, which rises more than 4,000 feet in less than 3 miles from the sea; historic Usal with its wooden bridge and gray-sand beach.

DIFFICULTY: Easy when dry; may become impassable when wet. Many blind curves. Keep to the right.

TIME & DISTANCE: 3 hours; 32 miles.

GETTING THERE: From the south, go north off Highway 1 onto Mendocino County road 431 at milepost 90.88, about 13 miles north of Westport and 14.7 miles west of U.S. 101. Watch for a "Narrow winding road" sign. From the north, at Redway or Garberville, go southwest toward Shelter Cove. Take either Chemise Mountain Rd. south from Shelter Cove Rd. or Briceland Rd. through Whitethorn to Four Corners. I start north of Westport and end at Shelter Cove Rd.

THE DRIVE: This tiny road snakes through the mountains on the most remote, undeveloped part of the California coast. Aptly nick-named the Lost Coast, it's one of the most isolated and wild segments of coastline remaining in the Lower 48. So daunting are these steep mountains of ancient seabed that Highway 1's builders were forced inland to terminate at U.S. 101 near Leggett. Before U.S. 101 was built in the 1920s, Usal Road was a vital link in the road system between Eureka and the Bay Area. Author Jack London and his wife, Charmian, traveled it in a horse-drawn carriage in 1911 on a trip to Eureka. After ascending the forested mountains, it enters the state park at mile 5.3, then descends to the rustic wooden bridge and mead-ows at Usal Creek. The turnoff to the beach is just north of the creek. At the beach are wharf pilings from the 1890s, when Usal was one of the North Coast's "doghole" lumber ports and mill towns served by steam-powered schooners. Usal remained an isolated village. Logging boomed again after World War II, but in a few years the big redwoods ran out. By 1960 Usal and Wheeler, another logging town farther up the coast, were abandoned. In 1969 their owner, Georgia-Pacific Corp., burned the surviving buildings to avoid liability problems. Usal Road ends 19 miles north of Usal, at the Four Corners junction. Here you can go southwest to Needle Rock and Bear Harbor *(trip 3)*. U.S. 101 is 22.5 miles to the right via Briceland Road and Whitethorn. Shelter Cove Road is 6.5 miles north, via Chemise Mountain Road. Gas up at Shelter Cove or Redway.

REST STOPS: Campgrounds, hiking, fishing at Usal. Two miles north of Westport on Hwy. 1 is Westport-Union Landing State Beach, a two-mile strip of coast with seven campgrounds. There are two campgrounds south of Shelter Cove Road (Wailaki is particularly nice; Nadelos has walk-in tent sites. Both are wheel-chair accessible.) Shelter Cove has all services.

GETTING HOME: Return to U.S. 101.

MAP: CSAA, *Northwestern California.*

INFORMATION: Mendocino Co.; Sinkyone Wilderness State Park.

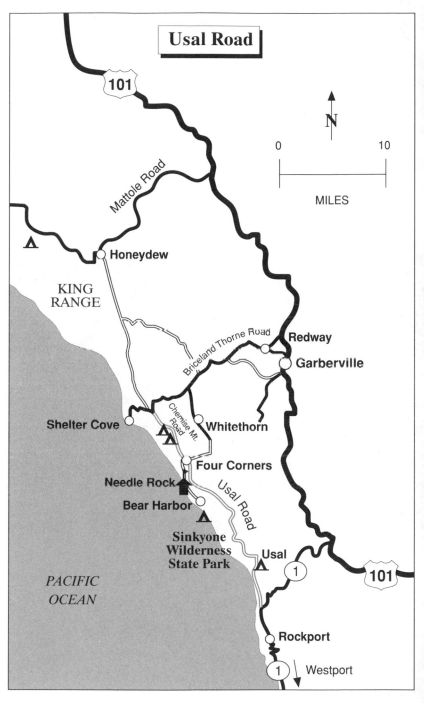

Usal Road

Bell Springs Road

LOCATION: Northern Mendocino County & southern Humboldt County.

HIGHLIGHTS: Fine vistas of picturesque farms, mountains and valleys. Elevation changes will range from 479 feet at Garberville to about 3,700 feet along the way. Since it begins and ends on U.S. 101, this road, much of which is one lane, is an outstanding opportunity to escape highway traffic for a while.

DIFFICULTY: Easy; a good dirt and gravel road.

TIME & DISTANCE: Two hours; about 35 miles from beginning to end at U.S. 101.

GETTING THERE: To go from south to north, take U.S. 101 about 12 miles north of Laytonville, in Mendocino County. As the highway curves left (west), Bell Springs Road will branch off to the right (north). From Garberville, drive north about 0.3 mile on Redwood Drive. Turn right (east) onto paved Alderpoint Road. After a little more than 10 miles veer right (south) at Harris onto Bell Springs Road. Set your odometer at 0.

THE DRIVE: I describe this drive from south to north, ending at Garberville. You will be at about 1,500 feet elevation when you turn north off U.S. 101, but in less than 4 miles this winding, twisting and narrow road up to Mail Ridge adds another 1,500 feet. There are deep canyons and coastal mountains to the west, and valleys and more mountains to the east as you zigzag through gorgeous scenery. By 12.5 miles begin a descent with panoramic views. At about mile 19.1 Island Mountain Road branches to the right. It's pretty, but it dead-ends in a little more than 7 miles. I don't think it's worth the detour. Pavement resumes in another 2.2 miles. Veer left (west) at the Y at Harris. It's 11 miles to Garberville.

REST STOPS: Laytonville & Garberville; Humboldt Redwoods State Park. Be sure to take Avenue of the Giants.

GETTING HOME: U.S. 101 north or south.

MAP: CSAA's *Northern California Section.*

INFORMATION: Mendocino County; Humboldt County.

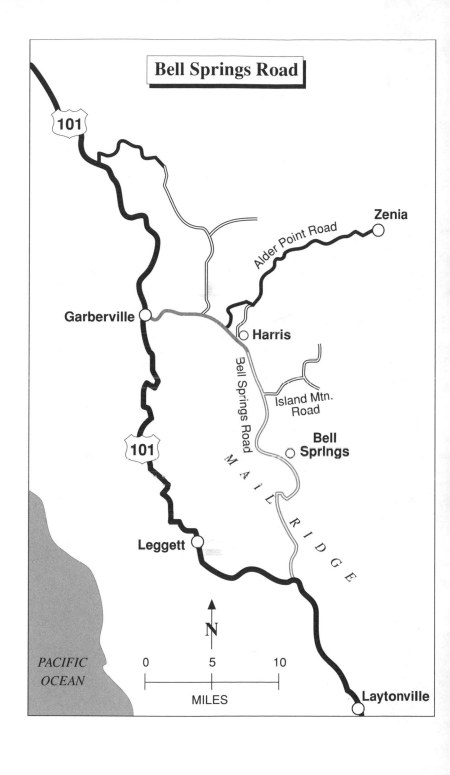

Bell Springs Road

101

Zenia

Alder Point Road

Garberville

Harris

Bell Springs Road

Island Mtn. Road

Bell Springs

101

MAIL RIDGE

Leggett

N

PACIFIC OCEAN

0   5   10

MILES

Laytonville

Fort Bragg-Sherwood Road

LOCATION: Mendocino County, between Fort Bragg on Highway 1 and Willits on U.S. 101.

HIGHLIGHTS: A remote east-west drive on a county-maintained road through rugged mountains between the coast and U.S. 101. Perhaps the most adventuresome motor route between the coast and inland areas.

DIFFICULTY: Easy to moderate. Watch for logging trucks.

TIME & DISTANCE: 2.5 hours; 42 miles.

GETTING THERE: You can begin off U.S. 101 at the north end of Willits (left at the light), or at Fort Bragg, on Highway 1. I start at Fort Bragg. From there, follow Oak Avenue east. Set your odometer at 0.

THE DRIVE: If you feel like you're in the middle of nowhere, it's because you are. This rudimentary, county-maintained route through logging country (note all the old redwood stumps) is one of the remotest roads in this book. Oak Avenue becomes dirt after 5.3 miles. At 6.5 miles you will come to a Y; keep right. Make a steep climb up a particularly narrow stretch. At 19.3 miles there's another Y; keep left. By about mile 26 there is finally a vista of the mountains and valleys to the west, and in another mile you will emerge from the forest into more open country. By mile 29 or so there are some farms, and then you will reach a T with a paved road. Sherwood Road continues to the right to Willits, about 12 miles farther.

REST STOPS: Willits and Fort Bragg have all services.

GETTING HOME: The coast highway or U.S. 101.

MAP: CSAA's *Northern California Section*.

INFORMATION: Mendocino County.

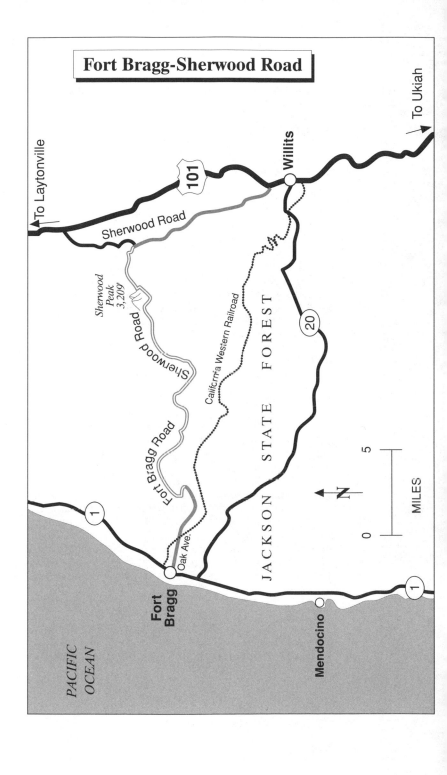

Fort Bragg-Sherwood Road

Fish Rock Road

LOCATION: Mendocino County, between Anchor Bay on the coast and state Highway 128 north of Yorkville.

HIGHLIGHTS: A very pretty route between the coast and U.S. 101.

DIFFICULTY: Couldn't be easier.

TIME & DISTANCE: About 25 miles and 1.5 hours between Iverson Road overlooking the coast and Highway 128.

GETTING THERE: From Cloverdale, on U.S. 101, take Highway 128 about 17 miles northwest to the Mailliard Redwoods State Reserve, and turn west. From Anchor Bay, take Fish Rock Road east to Iverson Road; go left (north) on Iverson Road for a short distance, then right (east) where Fish Rock Road resumes. From Gualala, south of Anchor Bay, take Iverson Road to Fish Rock Road. I begin at Highway 128 and go west. Set your odometer at 0.

THE DRIVE: One of the best features of this drive is getting there, through the idyllic countryside along Highway 128. The pavement ends 9.4 miles from the highway, after you pass through Mailliard Redwoods State Reserve. It's a pretty, relaxing and civilized cruise, to the sound of FM jazz if you wish, on a well-graded dirt and gravel road through mountains and valleys. By 18.4 miles the road narrows and becomes somewhat rocky as you begin a steep climb. (Four-wheel drive will help you avoid spinning your rear tires.) At mile 18.9 is a pullout with an outstanding view of waves of inland mountains and valleys to the north and east. By mile 19.7 you're at a summit, at about 2,300 feet. Soon you will have glimpses of the ocean through the trees on the left. By mile 23.4 pavement resumes. The descent is steep here. At mile 25.3 is Iverson Road. Offshore from Anchor Bay are Fish Rocks, a nesting place for many types of birds where you might also see seals and sea lions. Left or right on Iverson Road will take you to the coast highway.

REST STOPS: Mailliard Redwoods State Reserve, 3.2 miles west of Highway 128, has 242 acres of old-growth and second-growth trees. The sandy beach and tidepools at Fish Rock Beach are reached through privately run Anchor Bay Campground.

GETTING HOME: U.S. 101 or the coast highway.

MAP: CSAA's *Northern California Section.*

INFORMATION: Mendocino County.

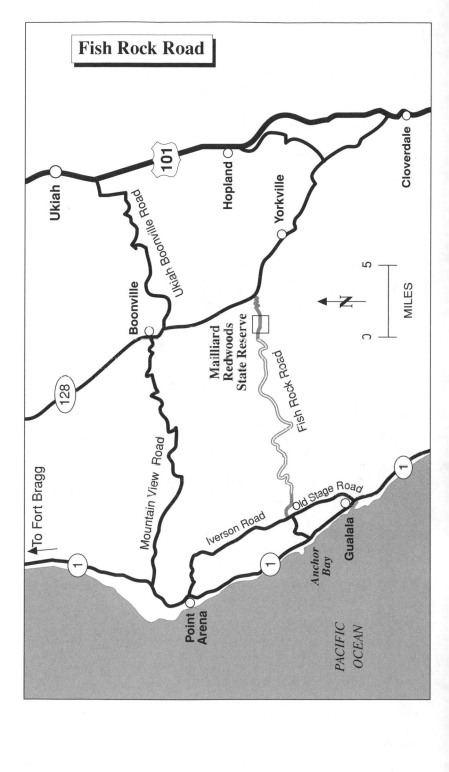

Fish Rock Road

Old Coast Road

LOCATION: Northern Big Sur Coast along Highway 1, south of Monterey. Goes between Bixby Landing and Andrew Molera State Park.

HIGHLIGHTS: A wonderful drive through coastal forest complete with moss-draped trees, ferns and gurgling brooks. A peaceful and beautiful alternative, if only for a short distance, to the traffic on Highway 1.

DIFFICULTY: Easy on a good, often one-lane dirt road. Occasional tight, blind curves.

TIME & DISTANCE: An hour; 10.2 miles.

GETTING THERE: If you're heading south on Highway 1, you will see the turnoff on the left at the northern end of that great arch, Bixby Creek Bridge. From the south, turn right off Highway 1 at Andrew Molera State Park. I start at the bridge.

THE DRIVE: First you will get the stunning view of the ocean and Bixby Creek Bridge, originally called Rainbow Bridge. When it was built in 1932, it was the highest single-arch bridge in the world, 260 feet high. You'll wind along a ledge in Bixby Canyon and quickly enter the rugged mountains. Climb a bit, then descend steeply into a deep canyon with lush vegetation. At 2.8 miles enter an enchanting forest of tall evergreens and rays of sunlight that cast a patchwork on the shaded roadbed. At mile 3.2, where there's a place to pull over and get out, you will feel cool and damp coastal breezes passing like a whisper through the trees as a brook gurgles nearby. Poet Lawrence Ferlinghetti had a cabin in Bixby Canyon that was frequented by Beat Generation writers in the late 1950s, including Jack Kerouac, who described his visits in his novel *Big Sur*. At mile 3.8 climb out of the forest and be greeted by sunshine and vistas of mountains and ocean. Then descend steeply, rounding a number of blind curves and crossing two one-lane bridges. Soon you're back on the highway.

REST STOPS: Primitive camping, hiking and fishing at Andrew Molera State Park.

GETTING HOME: Highway 1 north or south.

MAP: CSAA, *Monterey Bay Region*.

INFORMATION: Monterey County.

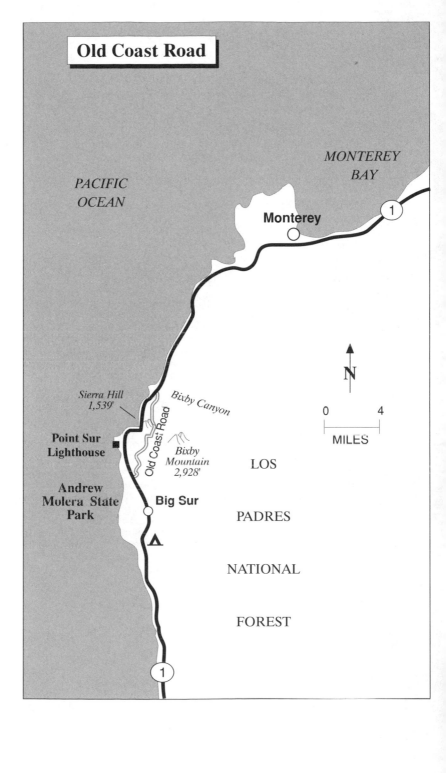

Old Coast Road

MONTEREY BAY

PACIFIC OCEAN

Monterey

1

N

Sierra Hill
1,539'

Bixby Canyon

Old Coast Road

0   4
MILES

Point Sur
Lighthouse

Bixby
Mountain
2,928'

LOS

Andrew
Molera State
Park

Big Sur

PADRES

NATIONAL

FOREST

1

Indians Road

LOCATION: Monterey County in the Santa Lucia Range west of King City; a corridor through the Ventana Wilderness. The county-maintained road, No. 3050, also is known as Arroyo Seco Road and Indians Station Road.

HIGHLIGHTS: A spectacular drive on a serpentine one-lane road along the side of the gorge of Arroyo Seco (Dry Creek). Mission San Antonio de Padua (1771). Spring wildflowers. A rare chance to experience a wilderness in your SUV.

DIFFICULTY: Easy. Closed in winter. Landslides closed this road in March 1995. The expense of clearing the slides kept it closed through fall of 1996, and no date had been set to reopen the road. So be sure to call ahead.

TIME & DISTANCE: 2.5 hours and about 34 miles between Mission San Antonio de Padua and Arroyo Seco.

GETTING THERE: From the north, take Arroyo Seco Road west of Greenfield (on U.S. 101). From the south, take Jolon Road southwest from U.S. 101 at King City to Hunter Liggett Military Reservation headquarters and Mission San Antonio de Padua. Then take Del Venturi Road north to Milpitas Road; go left and it will become Indians Road. It also can be reached from Highway 1 via Nacimiento-Fergusson Road.

THE DRIVE: I start near the old Spanish mission (set your odometer at 0), but it is arguably more scenic taken in the opposite direction. At about 12 miles you will leave the military reservation and enter the national forest. This area is referred to as The Indians, after the Salinan Indians. After several miles you will see the turnoff to large rock outcrops that include caves and grinding holes. At mile 17.1 the pavement ends, at waterless Memorial Park Campground. Go right through a gate. A short distance farther, below and to the left, there may be a pretty little pool in the creek that the kids will enjoy. Pass through an area of exposed granite, and then enter the gorge. Climb from the canyon bottom on switchbacks, getting a great view of steep mountains formed by massive faulting and uplifting. By 25.4 miles you're winding along the edge of the canyon. Descend toward the canyon floor, and creep along a narrow ledge. Pavement resumes at mile 33.7.

REST STOPS: There are a number of campgrounds (might be waterless, however) as well as scenic turnouts. Arroyo Seco Day Use Area has a beach along the creek.

GETTING HOME: U.S. 101.

MAPS: Los Padres N.F.; CSAA, *Monterey Bay Region.*

INFORMATION: Los Padres National Forest, Monterey District.

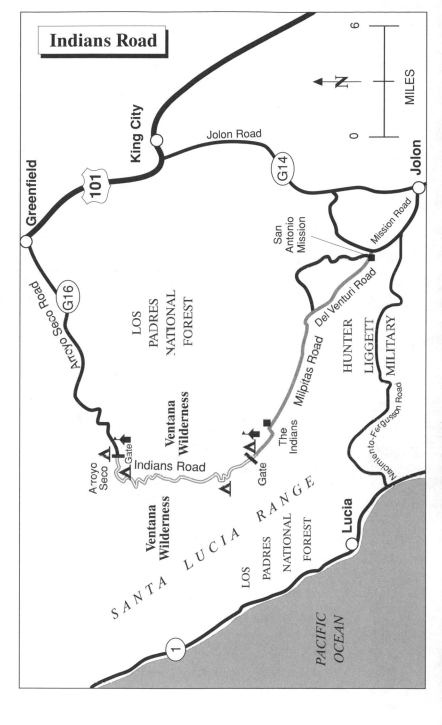

Cone Peak

LOCATION: Southern Big Sur Coast east of Highway 1, in the Santa Lucia Range, Los Padres National Forest.

HIGHLIGHTS: Readily accessible off the coast highway, this drive provides outstanding views of the ocean and interior mountains and valleys, especially from the 5,155-foot summit of Cone Peak, where there's a fire lookout. The peak is at the head of Limekiln Canyon, one of the steepest coastal canyons in the U.S.

DIFFICULTY: Easy.

TIME & DISTANCE: 2 hours and 27.2 miles round-trip. Add another 2.5 hours if you hike to the summit of Cone Peak.

GETTING THERE: Turn east onto paved Nacimiento-Fergusson Road about 4.1 miles south of Lucia on Highway 1. Set your odometer at 0.

THE DRIVE: You will start out at about 340 feet above sea level and drive to about 4,100 feet. Nacimiento-Fergusson Road winds steeply up into the mountains, providing stunning views of one of the world's most beautiful meeting places of land and sea. Throughout the Cone Peak Road segment you will be driving a route through the 250,000-acre Ventana Wilderness that is open to mechanized travel. In federal wilderness areas driving off such designated routes is illegal. At 3.9 miles, just as you enter the trees, there is a pullout with a brook that the kids will love to splash in. At mile 7 you will be at Nacimiento Summit. On the right is the start of dirt South Coast Ridge Road, a.k.a Coast Ridge Trail (20S05) *(trip 21)*. On the left is Cone Peak Road. It's a narrow road, a bit rocky in spots, that will give you even more fine views. At mile 12.3 you'll see, on the left, the Cone Peak trailhead. But continue another 1.3 miles to the end; it's quite scenic. There, hikers can access the North Coast Ridge Trail.

REST STOPS: Store and restaurant at Lucia; some primitive campsites and turnouts along the way; the summit of Cone Peak (a strenuous hike toward the end; carry water).

GETTING HOME: Highway 1 north or south.

MAPS: Los Padres N.F.; CSAA, *Monterey Bay Region.*

INFORMATION: Los Padres National Forest, Monterey Ranger District.

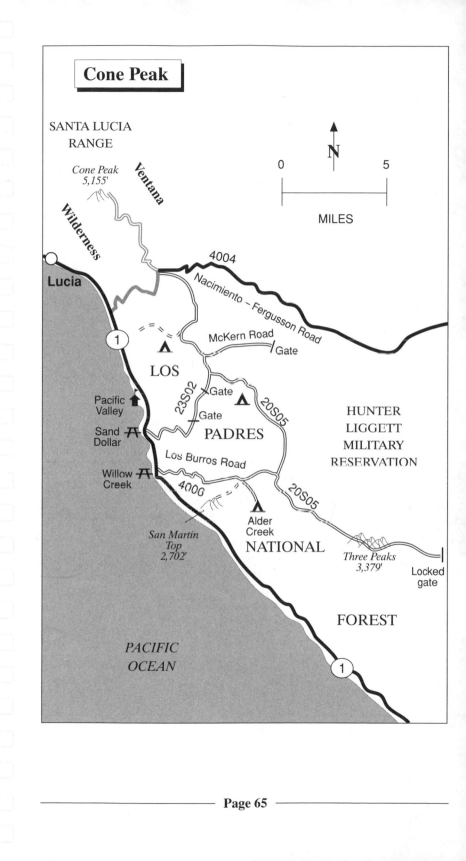

Cone Peak

SANTA LUCIA
RANGE

Cone Peak
5,155'

Ventana

Wilderness

Lucia

0   N   5

MILES

4004

Nacimiento – Fergusson Road

McKern Road
Gate

LOS

1

Pacific
Valley

23S02

Gate

Gate

20S05

PADRES

Sand
Dollar

Los Burros Road

HUNTER
LIGGETT
MILITARY
RESERVATION

Willow
Creek

4006

20S05

San Martin
Top
2,702'

Alder
Creek

NATIONAL

Three Peaks
3,379'

Locked
gate

FOREST

PACIFIC
OCEAN

1

South Coast Ridge Loop

LOCATION: Monterey County along the southern Big Sur Coast; Santa Lucia Range east of Hwy. 1 at Pacific Valley.

HIGHLIGHTS: A great side trip off Highway 1 that provides magnificent high-elevation vistas overlooking the coastline. If you have the time, this route can be combined with Cone Peak *(trip 20)*, San Martin Top *(trip 22)* and Three Peaks *(trip 23)*.

DIFFICULTY: Easy in dry weather.

TIME & DISTANCE: 2.5 hours; about 38 miles if you include two optional spurs.

GETTING THERE: If you're southbound on Highway 1, turn left (east) onto paved Nacimiento-Fergusson Road 4.1 miles south of Lucia. If you're northbound on Highway 1, turn right onto Los Burros Road, 4006, a half-mile south of Willow Creek Day Use Area (look for a narrow opening in the brush on the east side of the highway). I prefer the first way.

THE DRIVE: Nacimiento-Fergusson Road winds for 7 easy miles up to Nacimiento Summit. (There you can go left, or north, to Cone Peak.) Set your odometer at 0 here, and turn right (south) onto narrow South Coast Ridge Road, a.k.a. Coast Ridge Trail (20S05), which can be impassable in wet weather. You will cruise through coastal forest, getting occasional glimpses of the ocean below, as you climb to well over 3,000 feet. At about 4.4 miles Prewitt Ridge Road branches off to the right. It goes a short distance to an open area with excellent views and campsites (this area burned in October 1996, however-er). About 1.3 miles farther is the left (east) turn onto McKern Road. A dead-end road, it's still 7.1 fun and very scenic miles round-trip. A mile from this turnoff, on your right, is Plaskett Ridge Road. One used to be able to make a gorgeous descent on this road to Highway 1 at Sand Dollar Day Use Area. But it passes through private land, and has been closed to public access. (The Forest Service hopes the closure won't be permanent.) Continue south on South Coast Ridge Road for 8.1 miles, then turn right (west) onto Los Burros Road. On the descent to Highway 1 you'll pass the short but scenic route up San Martin Top and the historic mining district at Alder Creek Campground. You also could continue 6.4 miles (one-way) beyond the Los Burros Road turnoff to Three Peaks.

REST STOPS: Willow Creek & Sand Dollar Day Use Areas; Prewitt Ridge; Plaskett Creek C.G.; the hamlet of Lucia.

GETTING HOME: Highway 1 north or south.

MAPS: Los Padres N.F.; CSAA, *Monterey Bay Region* (the segment between Plaskett Ridge Road and Los Burros Road is not on CSAA's map).

INFORMATION: Los Padres N.F., Monterey District.

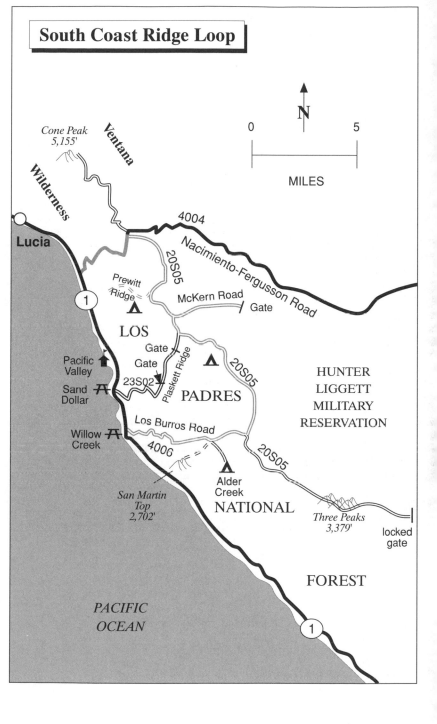

South Coast Ridge Loop

Cone Peak
5,155'

Ventana

Wilderness

Lucia

4004

Nacimiento-Fergusson Road

20S05

Prewitt Ridge

McKern Road

Gate

1

LOS

Gate

Gate

23S02

Plaskett Ridge

PADRES

20S05

Pacific Valley

Sand Dollar

HUNTER
LIGGETT
MILITARY
RESERVATION

Los Burros Road

Willow Creek

4006

20S05

San Martin
Top
2,702'

Alder
Creek

NATIONAL

Three Peaks
3,379'

locked
gate

FOREST

1

PACIFIC
OCEAN

0   5

MILES

N

San Martin Top

LOCATION: Southern Big Sur Coast in the Santa Lucia Range. Los Padres National Forest east of Highway 1 and southeast of Cape San Martin.

HIGHLIGHTS: More outstanding coastal views and easy access off Highway 1.

DIFFICULTY: Easy to moderate.

TIME & DISTANCE: 1.5 hours; 15 miles round-trip.

GETTING THERE: On Highway 1 about 4.6 miles south of Pacific Valley, or 0.5 mile south of the Willow Creek Day Use Area, watch for an opening in the brush and a cattle guard on the east side of the road. Turn east there, onto Los Burros Road, county road 4006.

THE DRIVE: Climb steeply into the coastal mountains and forest, preferably using 4wd to avoid tearing up the roadbed with spinning rear tires. The view along the way is great. At mile 5.9 is the intersection for San Martin Top and Alder Creek Campground. There are signs for each. Alder Creek C.G. lies within the historic Los Burros Mining District, where gold was discovered in 1887. Near the campground is the site of Mansfield, which was something of a boom town in the late 1800s, with 200 residents, a hotel, post office and five saloons. Fire destroyed it in 1909. Gold and silver were mined in the area until 1915. San Martin Top, el. 2,702, is west of the intersection; use 4wd as you drive along the ridge. About 1.2 miles from the intersection is a small Y; keep left. Soon you will reach a grove of trees. This is a good place to stop and enjoy the sweeping view, although the crude road continues down a bit farther. If you have the time, you can return to Los Burros Road and go right, climbing east 1.6 miles to South Coast Ridge Road, 20S05 *(trip 21)*. Going north along the ridge will take you to paved Nacimiento-Fergusson Road and Cone Peak *(trip 20)*. Going south will take you to Three Peaks *(trip 23)*, requiring back-tracking.

REST STOPS: San Martin Top; Alder Creek Campground; Willow Creek & Sand Dollar Day Use Areas; seaside Lucia.

GETTING HOME: Highway 1 north or south.

MAPS: Los Padres N.F.; CSAA, *Monterey Bay Region.*

INFORMATION: Los Padres National Forest, Monterey Ranger District.

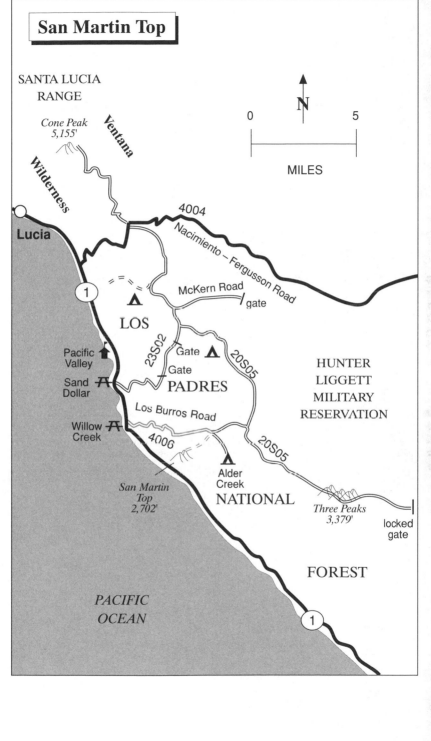

San Martin Top

SANTA LUCIA RANGE

Cone Peak 5,155'

Ventana

Wilderness

Lucia

0   N   5

MILES

4004

Nacimiento – Fergusson Road

McKern Road / gate

LOS

23S02

Pacific Valley

Sand Dollar

Gate A 20S05

Gate

PADRES

Los Burros Road

HUNTER LIGGETT MILITARY RESERVATION

Willow Creek

4006

20S05

San Martin Top 2,702'

Alder Creek

NATIONAL

Three Peaks 3,379'

locked gate

FOREST

PACIFIC OCEAN

1

Three Peaks

LOCATION: Monterey County on the southern Big Sur Coast in the Santa Lucia Range, Los Padres National Forest east of Highway 1 and southeast of Cape San Martin.

HIGHLIGHTS: Ridge-running high in the coastal mountains above Highway 1. Can be combined with the San Martin Top, South Coast Ridge Loop and Cone Peak drives.

DIFFICULTY: Easy.

TIME & DISTANCE: 2.5 hours; about 44 miles round-trip with the optional side trip to San Martin Top and the leg beyond Three Peaks.

GETTING THERE: On Highway 1 about 4.6 miles south of Pacific Valley, or 0.5 mile south of the Willow Creek Picnic Area, watch for an opening in the brush on the east side of the road. Turn there, onto Los Burros Road, county road 4006. If you're driving south on South Coast Ridge Road, continue for 6.4 miles beyond Los Burros Road.

THE DRIVE: Climb into the coastal mountains and forest, preferably using 4wd to avoid tearing up the roadbed with spinning rear tires. The view along the way is great. At mile 5.9 is the intersection for San Martin Top and Alder Creek Campground. Alder Creek C.G. lies within the historic Los Burros Mining District, where gold was discovered in 1887. Near the campground is the site of Mansfield, which was something of a boom town in the late 1800s, with 200 residents, a hotel, post office and five saloons. Fire destroyed it in 1909. Gold and silver were mined in the area until 1915. It's 1.6 miles farther to South Coast Ridge Road, 20S05, where you'll turn right. As you go south along the ridge there are dramatic views contrasting the misty ocean with mountains that seem to vault from the sea. East of the ridge is Hunter Liggett Military Reservation. Soon you will pass 3,499-ft. Lion Peak on the right, and then reach the cluster dubbed Three Peaks, which rise to 3,379 feet above sea level. Where the main road angles east, there's a badly eroded trail that continues south. Skip it. If you have more time, I recommend the 6-mile leg that veers down the east side of the ridge. It's scenic, but it ends at a locked gate to Hunter Liggett.

REST STOPS: Willow Creek & Sand Dollar Day Use Areas; San Martin Top; Three Peaks; various campsites along the way.

GETTING HOME: Retrace your route to Highway 1.

MAP: Los Padres National Forest.

INFORMATION: Los Padres N.F., Monterey District.

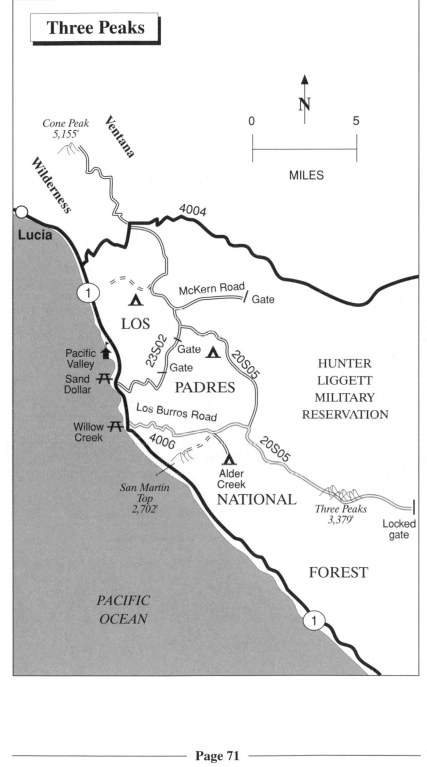

Three Peaks

Cone Peak
5,155'

Ventana
Wilderness

Lucia

4004

LOS

McKern Road / Gate

Pacific Valley
Sand Dollar

23S02

Gate
Gate

20S05

PADRES

Los Burros Road

HUNTER
LIGGETT
MILITARY
RESERVATION

Willow Creek

4006

20S05

San Martin Top
2,702'

Alder Creek

NATIONAL

Three Peaks
3,379'

Locked gate

FOREST

PACIFIC OCEAN

1

N

0   5

MILES

Cypress Mountain Drive

LOCATION: San Luis Obispo County northwest of Paso Robles.

HIGHLIGHTS: Outstanding vistas, pretty countryside.

DIFFICULTY: Easy.

TIME & DISTANCE: An hour; 10 miles.

GETTING THERE: Take state Highway 46 about midway between Highway 1 and U.S. 101. Go northwest on Santa Rosa Creek Road for 4.3 miles, then turn north onto Cypress Mountain Drive. (There may only be a sign for Adelaida.) Set your odometer at 0. You can also take pretty Santa Rosa Creek Road southeast from Highway 1 via Cambria for 12 miles.

THE DRIVE: The single-lane road immediately climbs steeply to 2,210 feet. As it winds up the mountains from a valley there are great views of the ocean, hills and valleys to the west. You will see lots of rock outcrops, as well as soaring hawks. By mile 1.2 the road begins to descend, and soon it meanders through woods high above ravines, eventually reaching a valley floor. Cross a cemented-over creekbed, and then a couple of quaint one-lane wood-plank bridges. At mile 6.3 is the inactive Klau Mine, where mercury was mined until the 1960s. Continue past Klau Mine Road for 3.3 miles to Chimney Rock Road. Continue north to Lake Nacimiento, or go east to U.S. 101.

REST STOPS: There are some wineries in the area. There also is a nice park in Paso Robles at Spring and 11th Street.

GETTING HOME: U.S. 101.

MAP: ACSC, *San Luis Obispo County*.

INFORMATION: San Luis Obispo County.

ALSO TRY: The fabulous 22-mile drive from La Cuesta Summit (on U.S. 101 north of San Luis Obispo) along Cuesta Ridge. Continue for 3 miles down an unmaintained dirt stretch to a permanently closed gate. (This segment is closed in wet weather.)

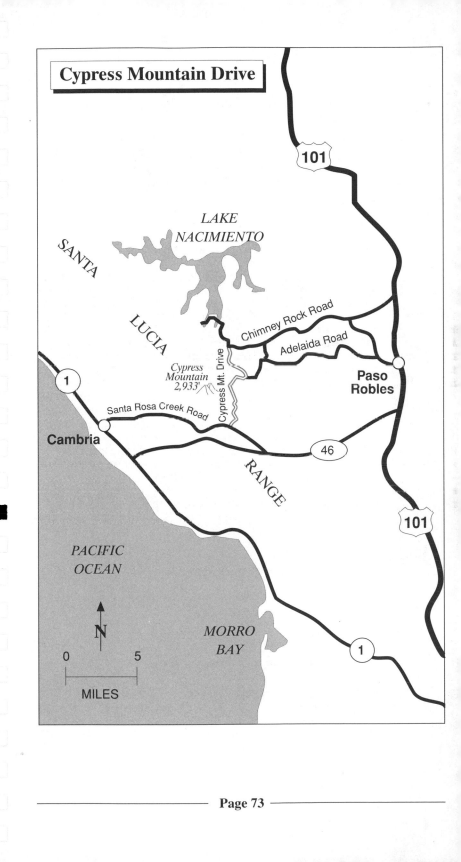

Cypress Mountain Drive

Santa Rita Road

LOCATION: San Luis Obispo County, between Templeton on U.S. 101 and Whale Rock Reservoir.

HIGHLIGHTS: What was it like to live in old California, when roads were narrow and dirt and you could watch deer graze and a humming bird hover among the flowers? This relaxing drive will take you back to that time, if only briefly.

DIFFICULTY: Easy one-lane road. Not advisable in wet weather.

TIME & DISTANCE: 1 hour; 14.7 miles.

GETTING THERE: From U.S. 101 at Templeton, take the Vineyard Drive off-ramp. Go west 0.5 mile, then turn left onto Santa Rita Road. From Highway 1, take Old Creek Road northeast 3.5 miles; turn right (east) onto Santa Rita Road.

THE DRIVE: I start off U.S. 101. Set your odometer at 0 when you turn onto Santa Rita Road. The first 4.7 miles are paved as you drive along an undulating country road beneath moss-draped oaks that provide a shading canopy. Soon the road emerges into a rolling landscape of oak woodlands and golden hay fields. When the pavement ends, the road becomes a single lane as it continues through woods. Suddenly, at mile 8, the road emerges from the shade into grassy hills bathed in sunlight. Cross a summit, at 1,557 feet above sea level, and take in a broad view of rugged coastal mountains and valleys. Pavement resumes at mile 13.5, and the road becomes two lanes again. In another 1.2 miles is Old Creek Road. You can go left toward the coast highway, or north to state Highway 46 and back to U.S. 101. If you want to see more of this lovely countryside, go across Highway 46 on Santa Rosa Creek Road to Cypress Mountain Drive *(trip 24)*.

REST STOPS: Templeton or Morro Bay.

GETTING HOME: Old Creek Road to Highway 1; U.S. 101 north or south.

MAP: ACSC, *San Luis Obispo County*.

INFORMATION: San Luis Obispo County.

ALSO TRY: The fabulous 22-mile drive from La Cuesta Summit (on U.S. 101 north of San Luis Obispo) along Cuesta Ridge. Continue for 3 miles down an unmaintained dirt stretch to a permanently closed gate. (This segment is closed in wet weather.)

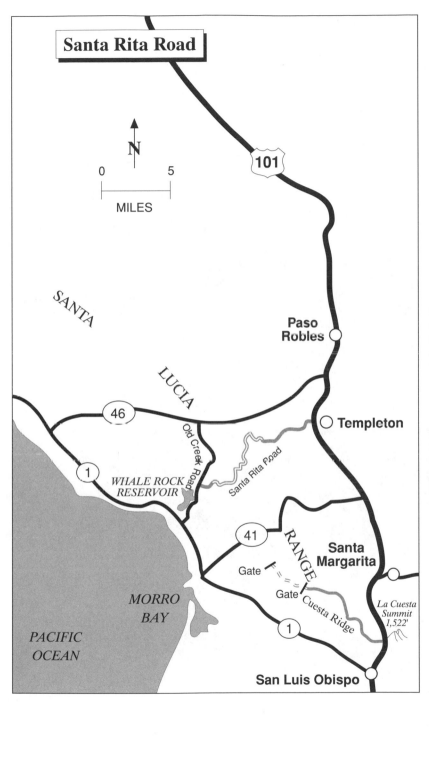

Santa Rita Road

Bear Harbor *(trip 3)*

Bear River Ridge Road *(trip 7)*

Windy Point (Punta Gorda, *trip 9*)

Punta Gorda lighthouse *(trip 9)*

King Range, Horse Mountain spur *(trip 13, Saddle Mountain Road)*

Usal Creek bridge, on Usal Road *(trip 14)*

Santa Rita Road *(trip 25)*

West Camino Cielo *(trip 32)*

Cuesta Ridge *(see trips 24, 25, 26, 27)*

Three Peaks *(trip 23)*

Never blaze your own trail, or follow the tracks of someone who did.

Big Caliente Hot Spring *(trip 33)*

Camuesa Road *(trip 33)*

Rincon Road, San Gabriel Canyon *(trip 41)*

Hi Mountain

LOCATION: San Luis Obispo County, east of Lopez Lake. Partly in Los Padres National Forest.

HIGHLIGHTS: Oak woodlands; vistas of the Santa Lucia Range. The road goes between the Santa Lucia and Garcia Wilderness areas, where mechanized travel isn't allowed.

DIFFICULTY: Easy. The first 6.1 miles are paved. The road to Pozo is often closed in winter by mud and high flows in the Salinas River.

TIME & DISTANCE: 1.5 hours; 34 miles.

GETTING THERE: From Arroyo Grande, on U.S. 101, drive to Lopez Lake. Cross the dam; 2.4 miles beyond it you'll see the sign for Hi Mountain Road. Set your odometer at 0.

THE DRIVE: The county road first winds along the edge of a marsh. At 1.8 miles the Arroyo Grande Ranger Station sits among grassy hills dotted with large oaks. (This area is being developed, and there will be private property on either side of the road until you cross into the national forest in 11 miles.) By 5.6 miles begin to wind up into the mountains, and soon the pavement will end. Here drive along a ledge above a ravine on a one-lane road with many blind curves. As you pass through a shady oak forest the road, 30S05, will cross the bed of Salt Creek repeatedly. Not far beyond the national forest boundary is an intersection. Road 30S05 to Pozo, your exit route, will be to the right. But go left (west) toward Hi Mountain Campground on road 30S11. This is a good mountain biking road, by the way, that dead-ends at the Santa Lucia Wilderness after about 9 miles. Take the short detour up to the lookout atop 3,180-foot Hi Mountain for a top-of-the-world vista. Continue along the ridge on the eastern edge of the wilderness. Backtrack to the intersection and continue to Pozo.

REST STOPS: The lookout. Hi Mountain Campground is pretty but waterless. Rustic Pozo Saloon & Restaurant.

GETTING HOME: Go west from Pozo to Santa Margarita.

MAPS: Los Padres N.F.; ACSC, *San Luis Obispo County*.

INFORMATION: Los Padres N.F., Santa Lucia District.

ALSO TRY: The 22-mile drive from La Cuesta Summit (on U.S. 101 north of San Luis Obispo) on Cuesta Ridge. Continue for 3 miles down an unmaintained dirt stretch to a permanently closed gate. (This segment is closed in wet weather.)

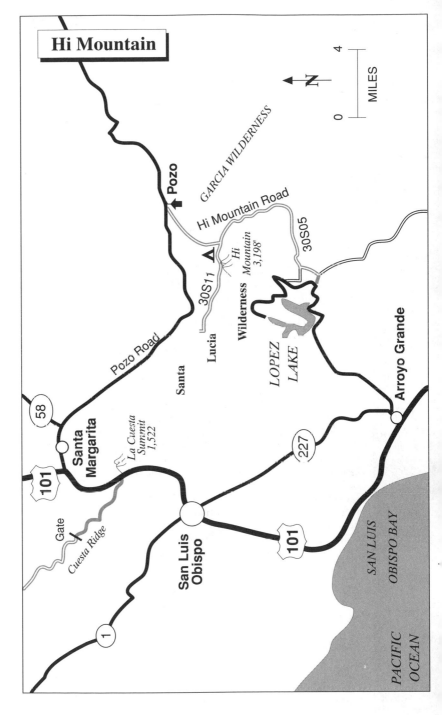

Hi Mountain

Avenales Observation Point

LOCATION: San Luis Obispo County. East of Arroyo Grande in Los Padres National Forest.

HIGHLIGHTS: Great view from a hilltop, at about 2,700 feet, that was a World War II civil defense post where a husband-wife team watched for enemy aircraft. Spring wildflowers.

DIFFICULTY: Easy. Closed in winter. The narrow, brushy road to Avenales Observation Point is moderate. There is a lot of private land in this area; refer to your Forest Service map.

TIME & DISTANCE: 4 hours. 50 miles round-trip from Lopez Drive (a.k.a. Lopez Lake Road, east of Arroyo Grande).

GETTING THERE: About 1.6 miles from the intersection of state Highway 227 and Lopez Drive, turn right (east) onto Huasna Road at a white bridge. Set your odometer at 0 there.

THE DRIVE: Follow the signs to the Huasna area. At mile 12.7, after winding through a pretty valley, cross a wooden one-lane bridge over the Huasna River. The dirt road begins on the other side. At 13.5 miles is a Y; veer right. The road will enter an oak woodland with grazing cattle. By about 22 miles, at a Y just before you cross into the national forest, you may see a sign for Agua Escondido and Stony Creek. Go left (north) on road 30S02. The road narrows as it runs along a ledge overlooking a valley. At about mile 23, as you go up a ravine, you will pass former Agua Escondido Campground. A mile farther, on the left, is road 19a, the spur to Avenales Observation Point. Use 4wd. It's 1.5 miles (one-way) to the overlook.

REST STOPS: The point. Stony Creek Campground, site of a Depression-era Civilian Conservation Corps camp, is 2.8 miles beyond the turnoff. The owner of the land through which the road passes does not allow motor vehicle access to the campground, but you can walk or bicycle the 2.5 miles from the gate to the campground.

GETTING HOME: Return to U.S. 101.

MAPS: Los Padres N.F.; ACSC, *San Luis Obispo County*.

INFORMATION: Los Padres N.F., Santa Lucia District.

ALSO TRY: The fabulous 22-mile drive from La Cuesta Summit (on U.S. 101 north of San Luis Obispo) along Cuesta Ridge. Continue for 3 miles down an unmaintained dirt stretch to a permanently closed gate. (This segment is closed in wet weather.)

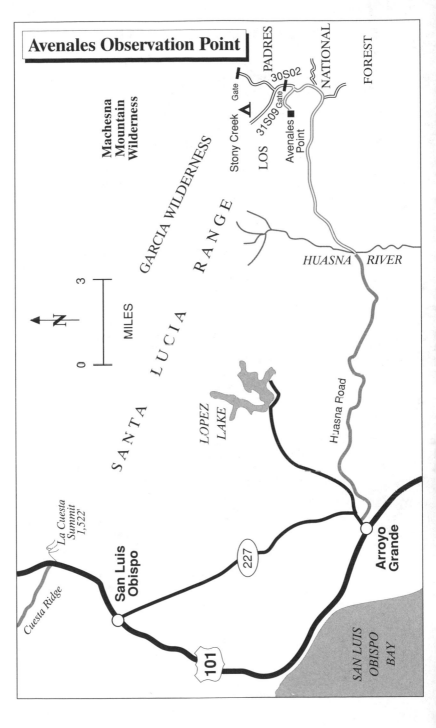

Avenales Observation Point

Machesna Mountain Wilderness

GARCIA WILDERNESS

SANTA LUCIA RANGE

PADRES

NATIONAL

FOREST

30S02

Stony Creek Gate

31S09 Gate

LOS

Avenales Point

HUASNA RIVER

N

MILES

0   3

LOPEZ LAKE

Huasna Road

La Cuesta Summit 1,522'

Cuesta Ridge

San Luis Obispo

227

Arroyo Grande

101

SAN LUIS OBISPO BAY

Sierra Madre Mountains

LOCATION: Santa Barbara County; Los Padres National Forest east of Santa Maria, on U.S. 101.

HIGHLIGHTS: Remote, rugged and gorgeous as you climb into the mountains, descend, climb, descend and then climb again to the truly breathtaking 5,000-foot crest of the Sierra Madre Mountains.

DIFFICULTY: Easy, but there are some rocky stretches and steep descents and climbs. A particularly well-marked route.

TIME & DISTANCE: 40 miles; 3 hours.

GETTING THERE: Take Tepusquet Road to Colson Canyon Road, county road 5543. Go east on Colson Canyon Road into the San Rafael Mountains.

THE DRIVE: At mile 5.1 is a summit with a view down into Rattlesnake Canyon. The road, 11N04 (closed in winter), snakes along the canyon wall. At mile 8.2 you're on the floor of the canyon. Cross the rocky streambed, and go left (northeast) on La Brea Canyon Road, which parallels North Fork La Brea Creek. (Here you might go right for 2 miles to the pretty Barrel Springs Campground area, where there is water occasionally.) Continue northeast on La Brea Canyon Road (still 11N04) toward Wagon Flat, crossing the streambed many times. Then climb out of the canyon to a ridge. At about mile 17.4 veer right onto Miranda Pine Road (11N03). At mile 20.2 cross a ridge, then begin a long series of switchbacks down into a deep valley at the northern edge of the federally protected San Rafael Wilderness (no mechanized travel is allowed). Then switchback up the opposite wall of the valley to Sierra Madre Road, 32S13, on the stunning crest of the Sierra Madre Mountains. (32S13 is open year-round.) To the west, the mountains are green with chaparral and woodlands. To the east, far below the ridge, lies dry Cuyama Valley and the Caliente Range, as well as the highest mountains in the Lower 48, the Sierra Nevada. To the southeast are the Tehachapi Mountains and, beyond that, the Mojave Desert. Go left (north) for 8.8 miles on the beautiful descent to Highway 166, or right to McPherson Peak *(trip 29)*.

REST STOPS: Refer to your map for campgrounds. Hiking and mountain biking in the Barrel Springs, Wagon Flat areas.

GETTING HOME: Highway 166 east through Cuyama Valley to Interstate 5, or west to U.S. 101.

MAPS: Los Padres N.F.; ACSC, *Santa Barbara County*.

INFORMATION: Los Padres N.F., Santa Lucia District.

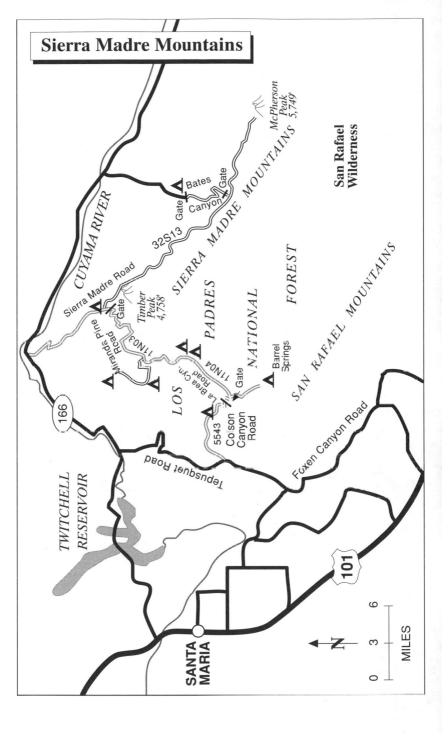

Sierra Madre Mountains

McPherson Peak Loop

LOCATION: Santa Barbara County; Sierra Madre Mountains east of Santa Maria; Los Padres National Forest.

HIGHLIGHTS: Great scenery along the climb to the mountains' 5,000-foot crest, and from the top of 5,747-foot McPherson Peak.

DIFFICULTY: Easy, but narrow and rocky in places.

TIME & DISTANCE: 4 hours; 51 miles from where you leave Highway 166 to where you return to it.

GETTING THERE: From U.S. 101 at Santa Maria, take Highway 166 east for 25.4 miles. Turn right (southeast) onto Sierra Madre Road, 32S13.

THE DRIVE: The road becomes dirt as you drive through hills of white oaks, starting at about 1,500 feet elevation. It's two lanes for the first 3 miles, but then narrows to a single lane with turnouts. The view of the Cuyama Valley, Caliente and Temblor ranges is outstanding. About halfway up, the road veers into the mountains, and you will get views toward the coast. By 8.8 miles you're on the ridge where Miranda Pine Road reaches the crest from the valley to the west. Ahead is a premier year-round ridgeline drive. At mile 22 you will pass your exit road, 11N01, Bates Canyon Road, on the left (often closed in winter). Continue for another 7.8 miles to McPherson Peak for superlative views. To the west, churning mountains green with chaparral and woodlands march to the sea. To the east, far below the ridge, lies dry Cuyama Valley and the Caliente Range. Far beyond them rise the highest mountains in the Lower 48, the Sierra Nevada. To the southeast are the Tehachapi Mountains and the Mojave Desert. From the peak, return to 11N01 and take it down the eastern slope toward Cuyama Valley. This narrow road winds down Bates Canyon for about 5.7 miles, where it becomes crudely paved Cottonwood Canyon Road near Bates Canyon Campground. The drive to the highway, across grasslands dotted with white oaks, is gorgeous.

REST STOPS: McPherson Peak; Miranda Pines & Bates Canyon campgrounds, both waterless.

GETTING HOME: Hwy. 166 to U.S. 101 or Interstate 5.

MAPS: Los Padres N.F.; ACSC, *Santa Barbara County*.

INFORMATION: Los Padres N.F., Santa Lucia District.

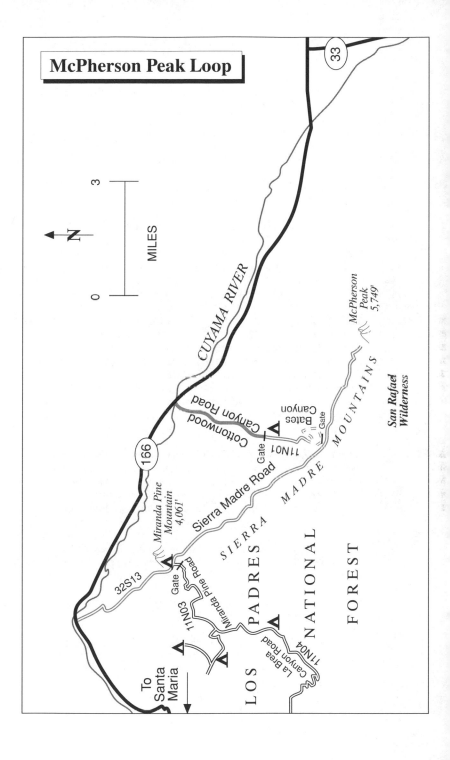

McPherson Peak Loop

MILES

N

3

0

CUYAMA RIVER

166

33

Cottonwood Canyon Road

Sierra Madre Road

Gate

11N01 Gate

Bates Canyon

McPherson Peak 5,749'

SIERRA MADRE MOUNTAINS

San Rafael Wilderness

Miranda Pine Mountain 4,061'

32S13

11N03 Gate

Miranpa Pine Road

La Brea Canyon Road

11N04

SIERRA PADRES NATIONAL FOREST

LOS

To Santa Maria

TRIP

30

San Emigdio Mountain

LOCATION: Ventura County, in the Sierra Madre Mountains west of I-5; Los Padres National Forest.

HIGHLIGHTS: One of the most spectacular vistas anywhere in the coastal mountains (looking inland) will greet you after a short drive through a forest of huge pines.

DIFFICULTY: Easy. One spot that can be slick when wet. Dead-ends.

TIME & DISTANCE: 40 minutes; 6.6 miles round-trip.

GETTING THERE: From I-5, take the Frazier Park exit. Go west 20.6 miles through Lake of the Woods and Pine Mountain Club, on Mil Potrero Road. Just past the Forest Service's Apache Canyon fire station turn right (north) on road 9N52.

THE DRIVE: Once again, we learn that beauty has nothing to do with the length, remoteness or roughness of a drive. This is a very pleasant climb through a forest of tall Jeffrey pine much like what you see in the Sierra. The road is steep at first, but levels out when you reach the crest of a ridge. At mile 3.3 is a turnaround with a truly stunning view, from 7,495 feet, across precipitous canyons and the southern end of the San Joaquin Valley to the southern Sierra. When you finish this drive, take the drive down Quatal Canyon, described separately.

REST STOPS: Kern County's nearby Mil Potrero Park (fee required) has camping (hot water, showers) and day-use facilities. Toad Spring Campground is nearby, on Quatal Canyon Road. At Frazier Park there's also Kern County's Frazier Mountain Park with a fishing pond, tables, shade and playground. Village of Pine Mountain Club.

GETTING HOME: I-5. Or you can take the Quatal Canyon drive (described separately) to Highway 33, and then go north to Highway 166 or south to U.S. 101 at Ventura.

MAPS: Los Padres National Forest; ACSC's *"Explore!"* map, *Ventura County*.

INFORMATION: Los Padres National Forest, Mt. Pinos Ranger District; Mil Potrero Park.

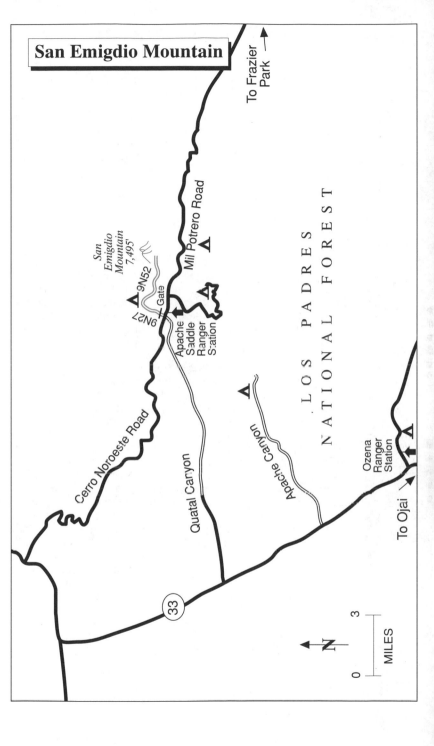

San Emigdio Mountain

To Frazier Park →

Mil Potrero Road

San Emigdio Mountain 7,495'

9N52

9N6

Gate

9N27

Apache Saddle Ranger Station

LOS PADRES NATIONAL FOREST

Cerro Noroeste Road

Quatal Canyon

Apache Canyon

Ozena Ranger Station

To Ojai

33

N

0 — 3

MILES

Quatal Canyon

LOCATION: Ventura County, in the Sierra Madre Mountains west of I-5; Los Padres National Forest.

HIGHLIGHTS: Although you're at the southern end of the South Coast Ranges, the aridity of the climate here, the washes up side canyons and the colorful, eroded cliffs will give you a sense of what desert touring is like. A pretty and intriguing drive.

DIFFICULTY: Easy. Side canyons are moderate to difficult.

TIME & DISTANCE: 1 hour; 14.7 miles; longer if you explore side canyons.

GETTING THERE: To go east, turn east onto Quatal Canyon Road (9N09 on the Forest Service map) from Highway 33 about 8.8 miles south of Highway 166, or 17.2 miles north of Pine Mountain Summit. To go west, turn south onto Quatal Canyon Road from Cerro Noroeste Road about 21.5 miles west of I-5 near Frazier Park. I go east, starting off Highway 33. Set your odometer at 0.

THE DRIVE: There's a vineyard on the left as you drive on a very good, two-lane roadbed of dirt and broken pavement. By mile 1.5 you're in the national forest. At mile 4.7 Quatal Canyon Road passes a gravel pit to the left. The road narrows from here, the pavement ends and the hills and bluffs become more colorful and vegetated. At mile 6.2 is a 4x4 route to the left (north), marked No. 106. Take it a mile or so along a wash up a beautiful narrow canyon (good for mountain biking). Along the way, on the east wall, are eroded spires. This route becomes too rough, so backtrack. Quatal Canyon Road becomes a bit rocky as it undulates through the canyon. About 1.4 miles from that last side trip there's another, also to the left (north). About 0.6 miles up this canyon you will cross a small streambed and come to another group of colorful spires. Park and walk. Back on the main road, as you approach the end of Quatal Canyon the hills will narrow. Notice the colorful cliffs. Soon you'll emerge onto Cerro Noroeste Rd., Forest Road 95. The San Emigdio Mt. drive *(trip 30)* starts 0.9 mile to the east.

REST STOPS: Toad Spring Campground is near the eastern end of the drive. Kern County's Mil Potrero Park (fee required) has camping, hot water, showers, day-use facilities.

GETTING HOME: Highways 33 or 166, or I-5.

MAPS: Los Padres N.F.; ACSC's *"Explore!"* map, *Ventura County.*

INFORMATION: Los Padres N.F., Mt. Pinos District.

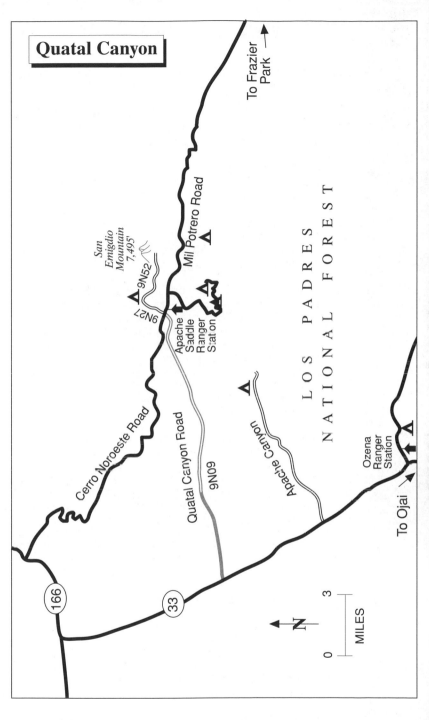

Quatal Canyon

To Frazier Park →

Mil Potrero Road

San Emigdio Mountain 7,495'

9N52

9N27

9N6

Apache Saddle Ranger Station

Cerro Noroeste Road

Quatal Canyon Road

9N09

Apache Canyon

L O S   P A D R E S
N A T I O N A L   F O R E S T

Ozena Ranger Station

To Ojai

166

33

N

0   3
MILES

West Camino Cielo

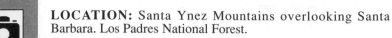

LOCATION: Santa Ynez Mountains overlooking Santa Barbara. Los Padres National Forest.

HIGHLIGHTS: Views of Channel Islands National Park and inland areas from a ridge that rises to 4,298 feet at Santa Ynez Peak. The gate to Ronald Reagan's ranch.

DIFFICULTY: Easy to moderate. Be prepared for poor road conditions. 5.6 miles of the western end, and 4.1 miles of the eastern end, are paved.

TIME & DISTANCE: 19.2 miles; 1.5 hours. If you add the beautiful northern leg of Refugio Road, starting or ending at Santa Ynez Valley, add another 7.6 miles and 30 minutes. (It's dirt for 1.3 miles below the pass.)

GETTING THERE: I take Hwy. 154 from U.S. 101 toward San Marcos Pass. 1.6 miles after Painted Cave Road turn left (west) onto Kinevan Road. Set your odometer at 0. West Camino Cielo, 5N19, begins in half a mile. You can also take the Refugio Road exit from U.S. 101, climb north for 7.2 twisting miles up to 2,254-foot Refugio Pass, and turn right (east) onto West Camino Cielo. You'll see signs warning that Santa Barbara County is not responsible if you drive this road. (At this point the northern leg of Refugio Road is directly ahead, dropping down into the forest.)

THE DRIVE: At mile 3.9 is a sign stating that the road is closed 14 miles ahead, but the gate was removed years ago. By 4.1 miles the road becomes one-lane dirt. There are some hairpin turns with great vistas. There are TV and radio facilities atop Broadcast Peak and an Air Force missile tracking station atop Santa Ynez Peak. Soon you will reach pavement, and then Refugio Pass and Refugio Road. Go left here, descending past the gate to Reagan's *Rancho Del Cielo* (the gate actually reads *Rancho Dos Vistas*) to U.S. 101. But go right, descending through an enchanting forest to Santa Ynez Valley.

REST STOPS: Santa Ynez wineries; the ersatz Danish town of Solvang; state beaches (with camping). Santa Barbara.

GETTING HOME: U.S. 101.

MAPS: Los Padres N.F.; ACSC, *Santa Barbara County*.

INFORMATION: Los Padres N.F., Santa Barbara Ranger District. Santa Barbara County.

ALSO TRY: Beautiful Figueroa Mtn. Recreation Area to the north, with its mountaintop lookout & spring wildflowers.

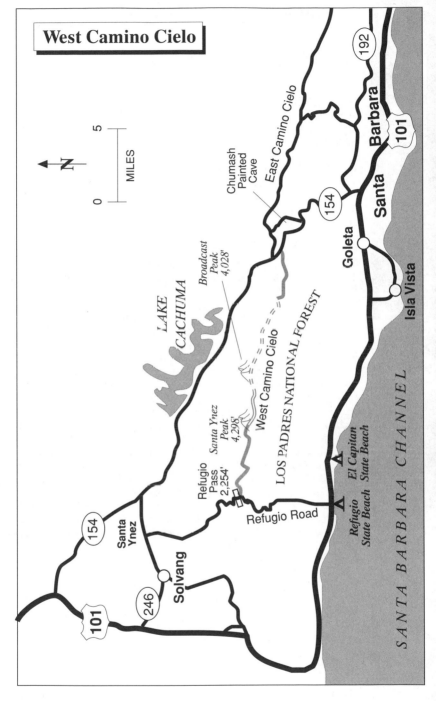

West Camino Cielo

TRIP
33

Big Caliente Hot Spring

LOCATION: Santa Barbara County, northeast of Santa Barbara in Los Padres National Forest.

HIGHLIGHTS: Spectacular, though paved, drive up to and along the crest of the Santa Ynez Mountains; lovely drive through inland valleys and woodlands. Chumash Painted Cave State Park.

DIFFICULTY: Easy. But the route was damaged by winter storms in 1994-95, and remained closed in spring. Call ahead.

TIME & DISTANCE: 5-6 hours, with time at the hot spring; about 60 miles round-trip.

GETTING THERE: From U.S. 101, take Highway 154 northwest of Santa Barbara 5.6 miles toward San Marcos Pass. Turn right (north) onto winding and paved Painted Cave Road. Set your odometer at 0.

THE DRIVE: Paved Painted Cave Road is a great drive, narrow with hairpin turns high above Santa Barbara, but it has been closed in the past by rain damage. At about 1.9 miles Painted Cave is on the left, just as you enter the trees. The cave contains beautiful pictographs, or rock art, painted by Chumash Indians. Continue climbing to East Camino Cielo, then go right (east). The road undulates along the crest on a picturesque paved road, 5N12 on the Forest Service map. Eventually on the right is the road down Rattlesnake Canyon, 5N25. (You can take this 7 miles to Santa Barbara on the return drive.) The pavement on East Camino Cielo ends in another 6.7 miles. The one-lane road turns inland and makes an exciting descent into the valley of the Santa Ynez River. Angle left (northwest) on Camuesa Road, 5N15. At Pendola Ranger Station angle right (north) on 5N16. (You may find the left fork closed to protect endangered frog, toad and turtle species.) Drive north up Agua Caliente (Hot Water) Canyon, cross paved streambeds several times (they can be slick) in a lush riparian area, and then you'll reach the spring and picnic area.

REST STOPS: Painted Cave. The hot spring, where you will find toilets and a picnic table. Regional campgrounds, including state beaches. Santa Barbara and vicinity have it all.

GETTING HOME: U.S. 101.

MAPS: Los Padres N.F.; ACSC, *Santa Barbara County.*

INFORMATION: Los Padres N.F., Santa Barbara Ranger District.

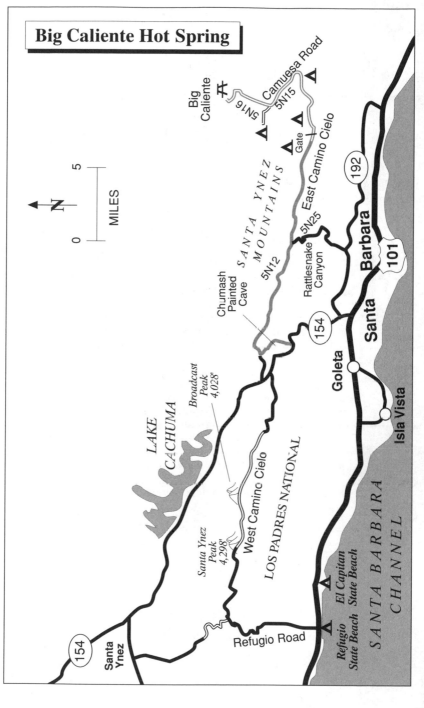

Big Caliente Hot Spring

Grade Valley

LOCATION: West of I-5, southwest of Frazier Park; Los Padres National Forest.

HIGHLIGHTS: Pretty valley; creek crossings; rock formations.

DIFFICULTY: Easy. A dead-end. Closed from the first snowfall in November until it's opened in spring, before Memorial Day weekend if possible.

TIME & DISTANCE: 3 hours; about 27 miles.

GETTING THERE: Take the Frazier Park exit from I-5. Go west for 7 miles to Lake of the Woods, then go southwest on Lockwood Valley Road for 10.4 miles. At a bend in the road turn left (south) onto Grade Valley Road, a.k.a. Mutau Road, 7N03 on the Forest Service map. Set your odometer at 0.

THE DRIVE: After almost 3.5 miles of badly washboarded road you'll pass through a pine forest, then be greeted with a view of beautiful Grade Valley. Notice the cliffs off to the left. Soon the road becomes narrow with loose rock as you descend. Note the seabed and lakebed sediments in the wall of the road cut. By mile 6 you're passing through pines (watch out for cattle). At mile 7, as you drive along a creek, there are some interesting sedimentary rock formations — layered, rounded and eroded. Veer left soon toward Mutau Flat. Cross Piru Creek if it's not running high and fast. For a pretty sidetrip, turn off the main road toward Half Moon Campground. Pass the campground and continue straight, past the willows. Follow Piru Creek Trail (7N13) for 2.3 easy miles (one-way) through a valley, past grassy meadows and stands of tall Jeffrey Pines. You may have to cross Piru Creek a few times. The road becomes a motorcycle route; you will have to turn back. Grade Valley Road ends 1.3 miles from Half Moon.

REST STOPS: Three campgrounds. Hike 7 miles (one-way) to Fishbowls, large stream-filled bowls in the sandstone.

GETTING HOME: I-5; Lockwood Valley Road west to Highway 33.

MAPS: Los Padres N.F.; ACSC's *Explore!* map for *Ventura County.*

INFORMATION: Los Padres N.F., Mt. Pinos District.

ALSO TRY: West Frazier Mine Road, a 4x4 route through old mining areas. This scenic drive starts at Lockwood Creek on road 8N12. Go left at the gate. Private property blocks access to Lockwood Valley Road, so take West Frazier Tie Road up to Frazier Mountain (there is a steep stretch), and exit via 8N04 at Chuchupate Ranger Station.

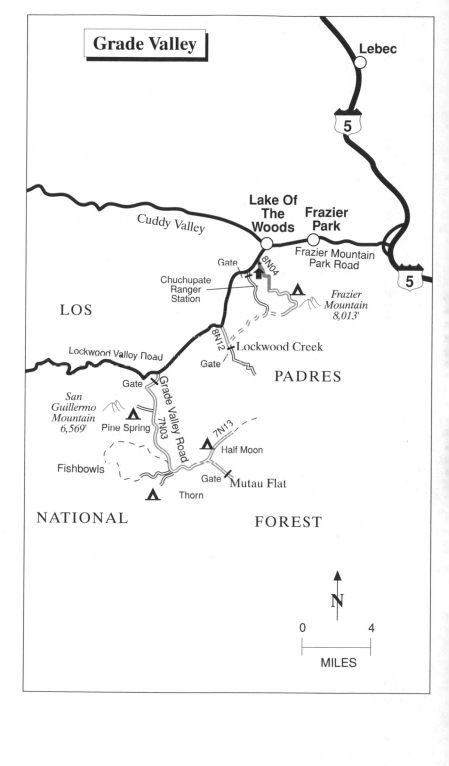

Grade Valley

Lebec

5

Cuddy Valley

Lake Of
The
Woods

Frazier
Park

Frazier Mountain
Park Road

5

Gate

8N04

Chuchupate
Ranger
Station

Frazier
Mountain
8,013'

LOS

8N12

Lockwood Creek

Lockwood Valley Road

Gate

PADRES

Gate

Grade Valley Road

San
Guillermo
Mountain
6,569'

Pine Spring

7N03

7N13

Fishbowls

Half Moon

Gate

Mutau Flat

NATIONAL

Thorn

FOREST

N

0   4

MILES

Alamo Mountain Loop

LOCATION: Ventura County, S.W. of I-5 & Hungry Valley State Vehicular Recreation Area. Los Padres National Forest.

HIGHLIGHTS: The beautiful climb up a piney, boulder-strewn mountain that rises to 7,455 feet, and the scenic loop around it. This is where the Transverse Ranges (in this case the Sierra Madre and San Gabriel mountains) meet the Tehachapis (geologically the southernmost extension of the Sierra) along the San Andreas Fault.

DIFFICULTY: Easy but slow. Narrow roads and many blind corners. Watch out for motorcycles, all-terrain vehicles.

TIME & DISTANCE: 2.5-3 hours, 44-53 miles, depending on whether you add the dead-end spur to Sewart Mountain, a worthwhile side trip with outstanding vistas.

GETTING THERE: Gorman exit from I-5. Follow the signs to Hungry Valley SVRA. Set your odometer at 0 when you turn off Peace Valley Road onto Gold Hill Road (8N01).

THE DRIVE: Pass the staffed fee collection station for the off-highway vehicle park that you must drive through. (National forest users like yourself don't have to pay.) Drive through an area set aside for off-highway vehicles. At mile 5.1 is a wooden fence rails; go right, as the sign indicates. From here wind through mountains and canyons on a one-lane, paved road. At mile 11.2 cross Dry Creek (which may not be dry). There's no bridge, but the creekbed is paved. The pavement ends at 13.2 miles, where you'll start climbing steeply. It's serpentine and somewhat rutted and rocky. There's a turnout at mile 15.9 from which you can take in the fine view. Soon you will be among tall pines. At 17.6 miles you'll reach a T, which is the start of the loop. Go either way; I take you right. Notice the pink hue of the granitic boulders. As you circle around the west side of the mountain, it becomes more heavily forested with tall pines that obscure the view, although there are occasional glimpses of distant coastal ridges. At mile 23.5 you'll reach the spur (road 6N10) to Sewart Mountain (8.2 miles round-trip). It'll take you on a ledge to the edge of the 250,000-acre Sespe Wilderness, with views as distant as the ocean on a clear day. The loop ends 3.2 miles beyond this turnoff.

REST STOPS: There are two primitive, waterless campgrounds on Alamo Mountain.

GETTING HOME: I-5.

MAPS: Los Padres N.F.; ACSC's *Explore!* map, *Ventura Co.*

INFORMATION: Los Padres N.F., Mt. Pinos District.

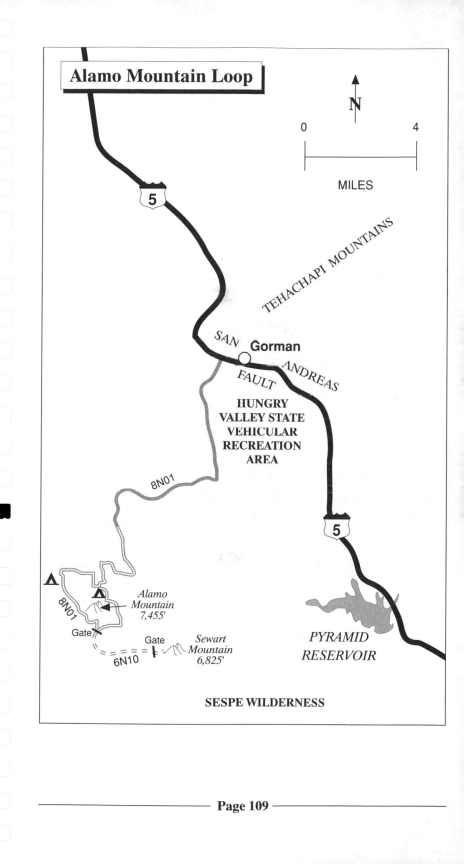

Alamo Mountain Loop

N

0   4

MILES

5

TEHACHAPI MOUNTAINS

SAN

Gorman

ANDREAS

FAULT

**HUNGRY
VALLEY STATE
VEHICULAR
RECREATION
AREA**

8N01

5

8N01

*Alamo
Mountain
7,455'*

Gate

Gate

6N10

*Sewart
Mountain
6,825'*

*PYRAMID
RESERVOIR*

SESPE WILDERNESS

Liebre Mountain

LOCATION: Los Angeles County, northeast of Pyramid Lake and east of Interstate 5. Angeles National Forest.

HIGHLIGHTS: Blockbuster vistas from yet another ridgeline road. Here in the San Gabriel Mountains, you'll be in the geologic and climatic meeting place of the southern Sierra Nevada (the Tehachapi Mountains), the Mojave Desert (Antelope Valley) and the South Coast Ranges. Although this road is some 50 miles from the ocean, it is in the east-west trending Transverse Ranges, one of the four geologic regions that make up California's coastal mountains. This drive provides views of the transition from churning coastal mountains to grassy hills and the arid Mojave Desert. Most of the road follows part of the Pacific Crest National Scenic Trail (hiking).

DIFFICULTY: Easy.

TIME & DISTANCE: Up to 3 hours; one option is 17.6 miles, another is about 24 miles.

GETTING THERE: Take Hwy. 138 to the eastern end of Quail Lake. Turn right (southeast) onto Ridge Route, road N2. Drive 2.2 miles, passing the intersection with Pine Canyon Rd. Continue another 3.1 miles on Old Ridge Road, 8N04 on the Forest Service map. Go left (east) onto road 7N23 toward Bear and Sawmill campgrounds. Set your odometer at 0.

THE DRIVE: Climb steeply through grassy hills, enjoying the fantastic vistas of rugged coastal mountains to the west. Using 4wd will help avoid spinning tires, which tear up the roadbed on this climb to well over 5,000 feet elevation. By about 4.6 miles you've reached the crest of Liebre Mountain, and the road becomes an easy, relaxing cruise. At 8.1 miles cross the Pacific Crest National Scenic Trail. Bear Campground at 8.4 miles. It's pleasant, with shading oaks. By 9.5 miles there is a stunning view of mountains, desert and valleys from 5,500 feet. At mile 11.7 pass the dead-end turnoff to the former Atmore Meadows campground. This road is closed in a couple of miles. Soon you will pass Sawmill Campground. At about mile 15.5 road 7N23 angles to the left (northeast). You can descend here 3.1 miles to Pine Canyon Road, or continue on 7N08 along Sawmill Mountain for 9.7 tedious miles to pavement near Lake Hughes.

REST STOPS: Waterless Bear and Sawmill campgrounds.

GETTING HOME: From Lake Hughes go northwest to I-5 or southeast to Highway 14.

MAPS: Angeles N.F.; ACSC, *Los Angeles Co. and Vicinity.*

INFORMATION: Angeles N.F., Saugus Ranger District.

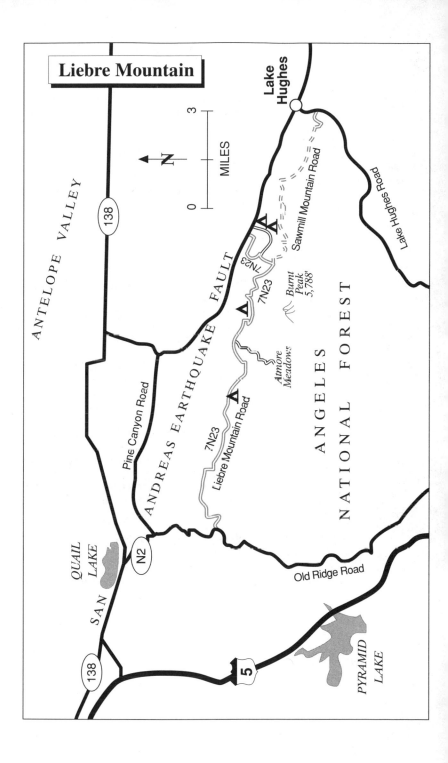

Liebre Mountain

Lake Hughes

ANTELOPE VALLEY

138

N

MILES

3

0

Sawmill Mountain Road

Lake Hughes Road

ANDREAS EARTHQUAKE FAULT

7N23

7N23

Burnt Peak 5,788'

Atmore Meadows

ANGELES

NATIONAL FOREST

Pine Canyon Road

7N23

Liebre Mountain Road

QUAIL LAKE

SAN

N2

Old Ridge Road

PYRAMID LAKE

138

5

Del Sur Ridge

LOCATION: Los Angeles County, east of Interstate 5 and Castaic Lake. Angeles National Forest.

HIGHLIGHTS: Excellent vistas from about 3,400 feet elevation in the San Gabriel Mountains, part of the coastal Transverse Ranges, although the semi-arid landscape is hardly what one thinks of as coastal. Most ridge routes go just below the crest, but this one puts you right on the crest overlooking Bouquet and Haskell canyons.

DIFFICULTY: Easy.

TIME & DISTANCE: 1 hour; 10.9 miles.

GETTING THERE: I recommend taking this going southwest for a better view. Southwest of Bouquet Reservoir, just beyond a bend in the road after some campgrounds, watch carefully for the turnoff to road 6N19, Quarry Rd., on the right (north). There is a sign, but it might be obscured by brush.

THE DRIVE: Immediately climb high above Bouquet Canyon as you approach this scenic ridge. Eventually angle left (southwest) onto road 6N18 (you will reach a gate if you go right). By mile 2.3 you're on the ridge. From up here you can see a varied landscape that includes mountains, canyons and valleys. It's a sweeping view that is missed by those who remain down in Bouquet Canyon. Follow the power transmission lines. At mile 8.7, as you descend, go left (south) onto road 5N24. (There is a locked gate on road 6N18 to Haskell Canyon, where there are some ersatz Western towns used as movie sets.) In another 2.2 miles you will come out on Bouquet Canyon Road.

REST STOPS: Check your Forest Service map for campgrounds.

GETTING HOME: Take Bouquet Canyon Road southwest toward I-5 and Highway 14.

MAPS: Angeles National Forest; ACSC, *Los Angeles County and Vicinity.*

INFORMATION: Angeles N.F., Saugus Ranger District.

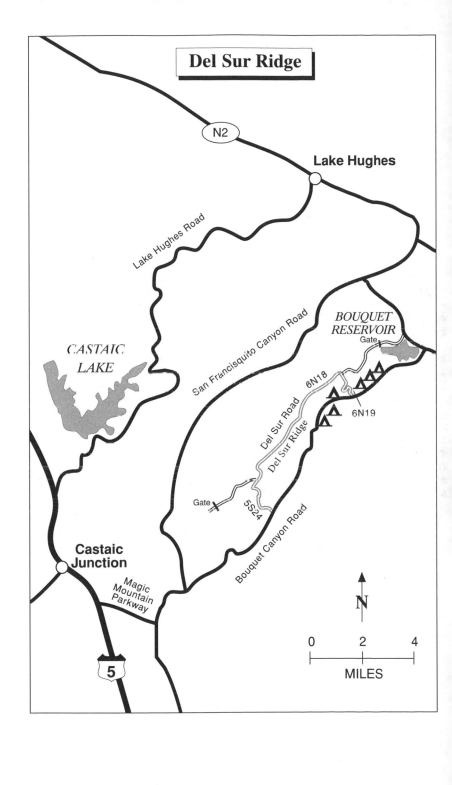

Del Sur Ridge

Magic Mountain Loop

LOCATION: Los Angeles County, between Interstate 210 and state Highway 14 (Antelope Valley Freeway) east of Interstate 5. Angeles National Forest, in the San Gabriel Mountains.

HIGHLIGHTS: A fascinating drive up Indian Canyon; a great vista at the top; a long, gentle ridgeline cruise to the end.

DIFFICULTY: Easy. Some might consider Indian Canyon almost moderate. About 6.4 miles of this drive are paved.

TIME & DISTANCE: An hour; 14.8 miles.

GETTING THERE: Take Soledad Canyon Road east; turn right (south) onto road 4N37 at the sign for Indian Canyon, near some private campgrounds. To go in the other direction, take Sand Canyon Road south from Hwy. 14 to Santa Clara Divide Rd., 3N17; or take Little Tujunga Canyon Road north from I-210 to Santa Clara Divide Road. I start at Indian Canyon.

THE DRIVE: The drive up Indian Canyon is steep, winding and narrow, but not difficult. Just sit back and let your 4wd system do the work. It's a scenic drive, too, with great views of desert lands to the northeast. The Indian Canyon leg parallels the Pacific Crest National Scenic Trail. Use the pullouts along the way to enjoy the view as you climb about 2,100 feet. In about 5.6 miles you will reach the top; go right (west) on road 3N17, Santa Clara Divide Road. You're at almost 4,500 feet elevation here. Drive west along the highly scenic ridge, past Magic Mountain and high above one deep canyon after another. San Gabriel Fault passes through this area. By mile 8.4, at Magic Mountain, the road is paved. But it's still a narrow, one-lane mountain road with some blind turns and fallen rock. Make a long, easy descent. At mile 14.8 you'll reach paved Sand Canyon Road, the end of the drive.

REST STOPS: There's an outstanding view from a pullout at the top of Indian Canyon. At the end of the drive, you can go left for about 50 yards to a picnic area at Bear Divide Vista, or right about 1.5 miles to Live Oak picnic area and campground. The latter have water.

GETTING HOME: Highway 14 west to Interstate 5 or east and north toward Lancaster. Or take Little Tujunga Canyon Road southwest to I-210.

MAPS: Angeles National Forest; ACSC, *Los Angeles County & Vicinity.*

INFORMATION: Angeles N.F., Tujunga Ranger District.

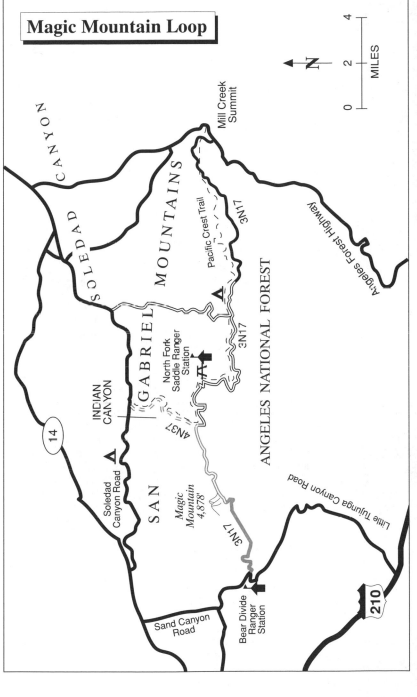

Magic Mountain Loop

Mill Creek Summit

SOLEDAD CANYON

SAN GABRIEL MOUNTAINS

Pacific Crest Trail

3N17

Angeles Forest Highway

ANGELES NATIONAL FOREST

North Fork Saddle Ranger Station

3N17

INDIAN CANYON

4N37

14

Soledad Canyon Road

Magic Mountain 4,878'

3N17

Little Tujunga Canyon Road

Sand Canyon Road

Bear Divide Ranger Station

210

N

0   2   4
MILES

Pacific Crest Trail

LOCATION: Los Angeles County, south of Soledad Canyon Road. Angeles National Forest.

HIGHLIGHTS: This high ridgeline route, Santa Clara Divide Road, parallels the Pacific Crest National Scenic Trail, and you don't have to hike! Magnificent scenery that includes countless deep canyons in the rugged San Gabriel Mountains. This route is popular for road rallies.

DIFFICULTY: Easy. Some might consider Indian Canyon almost moderate.

TIME & DISTANCE: 2.5 hours; 27 miles.

GETTING THERE: You can take this in either direction between Soledad Canyon Road (turn right, south, on Indian Canyon Road) and Mill Creek Summit on Angeles Forest Highway. I start at Mill Creek. Set your odometer at 0.

THE DRIVE: From the summit take narrow and undulating Santa Clara Divide Road, 3N17, which is paved for first 9.2 miles. The fine views range from interior desert to green mountains. After about 10 miles you've reached Messenger Flats Campground. It has tables and shade, but no privacy. Climb to well over 5,000 feet as you drive along the ridges. Then begin descending along a narrow ledge with a long, steep drop-off to the side. The scenery here is outstanding. At about mile 16 you'll reach a pullout with a spectacular vista of the mountains. At mile 17.5 is North Fork Saddle Ranger Station, which sits, as you might expect, on a saddle between mountains. Just beyond the station there are some steep, but paved, stretches. At mile 19.5 cross another saddle with stunning views of chaparral-covered mountains and canyons on your left and the vast Mojave Desert on your right (eastward). Soon you will see road 4N37 dropping down into Indian Canyon on your right (north). Take it to Soledad Canyon Road, 5.6 miles away. Or continue west along the ridge for about 9.5 scenic miles, passing Magic Mountain (where the road becomes paved) and dropping down to Sand Canyon Road.

REST STOPS: Refer to your Forest Service map for campgrounds and picnic areas. There is a pretty picnic area at North Fork Saddle Station.

GETTING HOME: Angeles Forest Highway southwest toward Interstate 210, or Soledad Road to Highway 14.

MAPS: Angeles N.F.; ACSC, *Los Angeles Co. & Vicinity*.

INFORMATION: Angeles N.F., Tujunga District.

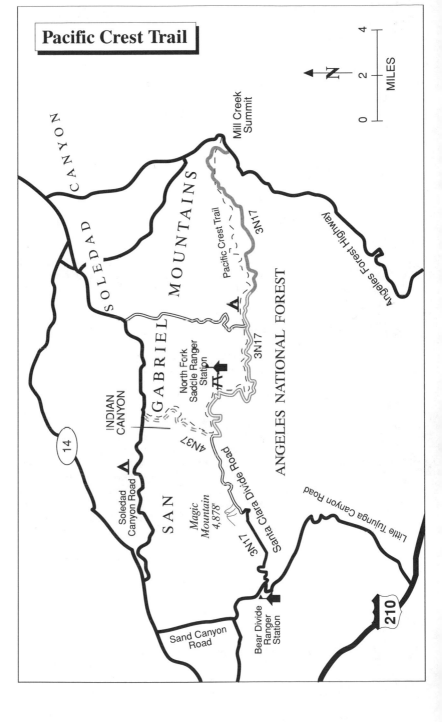

Pacific Crest Trail

Pacifico Mtn. to Little Rock

LOCATION: Los Angeles County north of Pasadena. East of Mill Creek Summit on the Angeles Forest Highway in the San Gabriel Mountains. Angeles National Forest.

HIGHLIGHTS: Beautiful Little Rock Canyon. Great vistas from Round Top (el. 6,316) & Pacifico Mountain (el. 7,124).

DIFFICULTY: Easy, but heavy rains in the winter of 1994-95 and a fire damaged this route and may have changed conditions. Call ahead. There are many blind curves on the one-lane road up Round Top.

TIME & DISTANCE: 2.5 hours or longer; 27.5 miles with side routes.

GETTING THERE: Take Angeles Forest Highway to Mill Creek Summit. You will see a picnic area. Turn south onto road 3N17, which is closed from about Nov. 15 to about May 15. Set your odometer at 0, and drive through the Los Angeles County maintenance yard. Or go south from Little Rock Reservoir on road 5N04. I start at Mill Creek Summit.

THE DRIVE: The vistas of Antelope Valley and the Mojave Desert are outstanding as you climb along a ledge. After about 3.3 miles you can turn right (south) on road 3N90 to Round Top, 2.7 serpentine miles away. Don't miss it. 1.3 miles beyond that turnoff, on the left, is the road to Pacifico Mountain. On the way up notice the damage done by irresponsible motorists who decided to make their own trails. The main road descends along a few narrow ledges, eventually reaching an intersection and a short paved stretch. Go left (east) toward Little Rock Reservoir on 5N04, passing the Pinyon Shooting Area. From here you will descend on an occasionally rocky road through Little Rock Canyon Recreation Area. About 6.8 miles from the intersection is Little Sycamore. Continue north toward the reservoir.

REST STOPS: The picnic area at Mill Creek Summit. Round Top and Pacifico Mountain. There's a campground at Pacifico with spectacular vistas of valleys below, tall pines and lots of granite boulders for the kids to scale. Little Sycamore is a nice place to let the kids play in Little Rock Creek. Camping at the reservoir.

GETTING HOME: From Little Rock go north to Highway 138. From Mill Creek Summit go southwest toward I-210.

MAPS: Angeles N.F.; ACSC's *Los Angeles Co. & Vicinity*.

INFORMATION: Angeles N.F., Valyermo District.

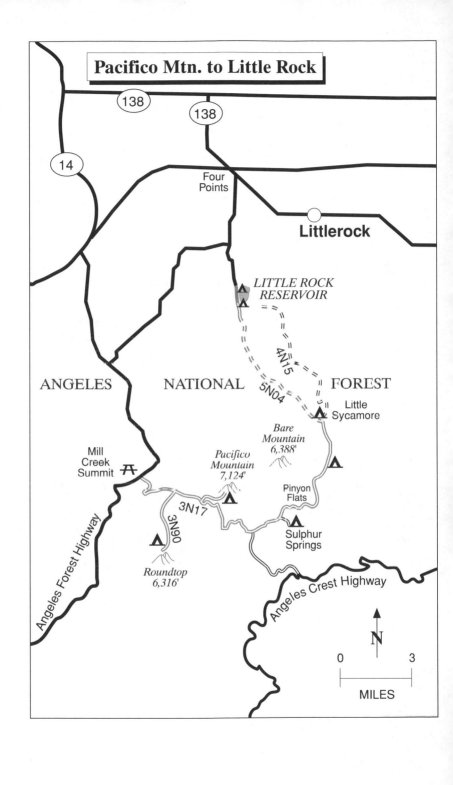

Pacifico Mtn. to Little Rock

138

138

14

Four
Points

Littlerock

*LITTLE ROCK
RESERVOIR*

4N15

5N04

ANGELES   NATIONAL   FOREST

Little
Sycamore

*Bare
Mountain
6,388'*

Mill
Creek
Summit

*Pacifico
Mountain
7,124'*

Pinyon
Flats

3N17

Sulphur
Springs

3N90

Angeles Forest Highway

*Roundtop
6,316'*

Angeles Crest Highway

N

0   3

MILES

Rincon to Shortcut

LOCATION: Los Angeles County, in the San Gabriel Mountains northeast of Pasadena. Angeles National Forest.

HIGHLIGHTS: Ridge-running on an exhilarating adventure road with astounding scenery. Glimpses of Mt. Wilson Observatory, where astronomers first realized the universe consists of more than one galaxy. (It was closed in 1985.)

DIFFICULTY: Easy but slow; be careful on this narrow road with steep drop-offs. Closed in winter. One-way only.

TIME & DISTANCE: 3.5 hours; 25.6 miles.

GETTING THERE: First get the combination to two locked gates the Forest Service uses to control use of the road, a designated off-highway vehicle route, for safety reasons and to limit damage. You must get the combination in person at the Mt. Baldy District Office in Glendora (the address and telephone number are listed in the back of the book). Insist that they double check it; it's changed regularly. Sometimes these locks are sticky, so bring a spray lubricant. Drive up San Gabriel Canyon Road. Just beyond the off-highway vehicle area you'll see the first gate on the left, on road 2N24. Set your odometer at 0.

THE DRIVE: This is the Rincon-Red Box Road. One used to be able to drive between the Red Box and Rincon ranger stations. Now there's a locked gate east of Red Box, and that leg is closed to motor vehicles. So turn north instead onto road 2N23 to come out on Highway 2 west of Shortcut Ranger Station. At the start, once you're through the gate make the breathtaking ascent into the steep mountains above San Gabriel Canyon. Creep along an easy but narrow and, for many, hairraising one-lane ledge. It's a good road otherwise. There's a large turnout at mile 2.4. From here you'll wind along a ridge that rises to almost 4,800 feet elevation by mile 11.7. The view on a clear spring day can include Los Angeles, Palos Verdes Peninsula, the ocean and deserts. By 16.9 miles you'll veer right (north) onto 2N23, and descend on a more primitive road into Shortcut Canyon. About 2.8 miles from the turnoff cross San Gabriel River. From here climb out of the canyon to another ridge. Soon you will reach the second locked gate at Highway 2.

REST STOPS: Many pullouts. Picnic area at Shortcut.

GETTING HOME: Take Highway 2 south to I-210.

MAP: Angeles National Forest.

INFORMATION: Angeles N.F., Arroyo Seco Ranger District; Mt. Baldy Ranger District.

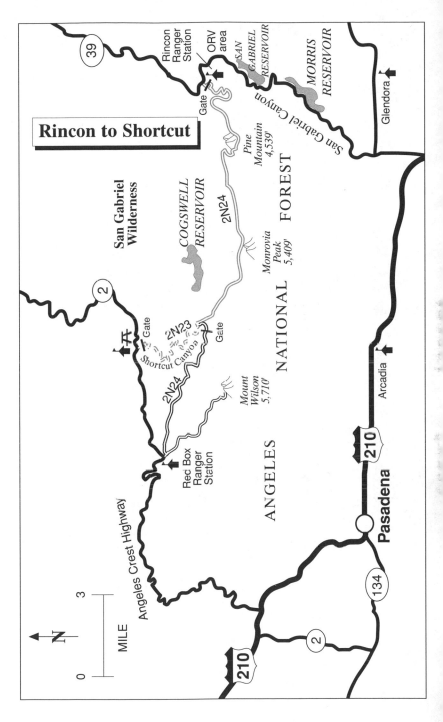

Rincon to Shortcut

North Main Divide Road

LOCATION: Southwest of Corona along the Riverside-Orange county line on the crest of the Santa Ana Mountains. Cleveland National Forest.

HIGHLIGHTS: Many pullouts from which to enjoy great vistas as you travel along a high ridge east of the Gulf of Santa Catalina.

DIFFICULTY: Easy. A few moderately rough spots. This route, particularly Maple Springs Road, may be closed by damage from winter rains. Be sure to call ahead.

TIME & DISTANCE: 4 leisurely hours; almost 30 miles from the Ortega Highway to Silverado Canyon Road.

GETTING THERE: Take Highway 74, the Ortega Highway, toward El Cariso Forest Station west of Lake Elsinore. Turn northwest onto Long Canyon Road (6S05) on the north side of Hwy. 74. Set your odometer at 0. (You can go in the opposite direction.)

THE DRIVE: The pavement ends after 4.3 miles near Los Pinos Spring, where the paved loop road meets North Main Divide Road (3S04). Heading north on the dirt road, it will be moderately rough in places as you wind up to Santiago Peak (5,687 ft.), 16.8 miles from Ortega Highway. Along the way you will have great views eastward toward the San Jacinto Mountains. You'll pass, on the right, the turnoff for Indian Road (5S01), which is often closed. There is a vista point among the 125-plus radio, TV and microwave facilities clustered atop the peak, which stands isolated from other major peaks in the Santa Anas. The road improves after Santiago Peak. You can see east and west from pullouts along the ridge. At about mile 21.4 you will see Maple Springs Road (5S04) branch off to the left. Take it. The first 4.5 miles of the descent will be on dirt; the next 4 miles will be paved. At mile 29.9 you'll reach Silverado Canyon Road.

REST STOPS: Anywhere you like along the way. Blue Jay is an unimproved campground; El Cariso is improved. Falcon is a group campground.

GETTING HOME: Take Silverado Canyon Road west to Santiago Canyon Road (S18). Take S18 northwest toward Highway 55 or south to Interstate 5 at Laguna Hills.

MAPS: Cleveland N.F.; ACSC, *Los Angeles Co. & Vicinity*.

INFORMATION: Cleveland N.F., Trabuco Ranger District.

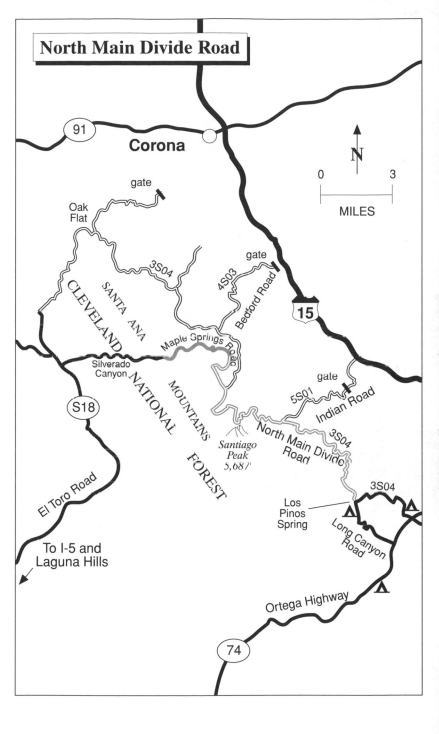

North Main Divide Road

91

Corona

N

0   3

MILES

gate

Oak Flat

3S04

4S03

gate

Bedford Road

15

CLEVELAND

SANTA ANA

Maple Springs Road

Silverado Canyon

gate

5S01

Indian Road

S18

NATIONAL

MOUNTAINS

Santiago Peak 5,687'

North Main Divide Road

3S04

El Toro Road

FOREST

3S04

Los Pinos Spring

Long Canyon Road

To I-5 and Laguna Hills

Ortega Highway

74

Wildomar Road

LOCATION: Santa Ana Mountains in Riverside County, south of Lake Elsinore. Cleveland National Forest. On some maps this route may be identified as Tenaja-Los Alamos Road.

HIGHLIGHTS: The waterfalls in spring; rugged, remote mountain and canyon scenery. Not far from Interstate 5. Hang gliders along Killen Trail/South Main Divide Road (6S07), along a ridge with blockbuster views about 1,600 feet above Lake Elsinore.

DIFFICULTY: Easy. You might be sharing the road with motorcyclists, so be careful and considerate. This road was damaged by heavy rains in the winter of 1994-95; call ahead.

TIME & DISTANCE: 3 hours; 21 miles.

GETTING THERE: You can start at Highway 74, the Ortega Highway, about 5.8 miles west of Lake Elsinore and go south at El Cariso Forest Station along Killen Trail/South Main Divide Road (6S07) to Wildomar Road (7S04). Or start at Tenaja Trailhead southwest of the town of Wildomar and take the drive north. I do the latter, reaching it via Clinton Keith Road south to Tenaja Road, then right (northwest) onto Wildomar Road (a sign may say Rancho California Road).

THE DRIVE: Drive along the eastern boundary of the San Mateo Canyon Wilderness, where mechanized travel is not allowed. At Tenaja you can see Indian grinding holes in nearby rocks. To see them, take the left spur past the cattle guard, before the trailhead parking area. The pavement ends at the trailhead, where you should set your odometer at 0. The road is a good, serpentine one-laner with pullouts from which you can peer down into Tenaja and San Mateo canyons. At mile 5.3 the road bends east. To the left is a parking area if you want to visit the waterfalls. At mile 6 cross a stream at an improved crossing, and for the next 100 yards or so the roadbed will be a bit rocky. By about mile 8 the road improves markedly. Soon you will start seeing private residences on the ridge to the right. At Wildomar Campground and the off-highway vehicle area the road becomes paved. Soon it bends northwest and becomes road 6S07.

REST STOPS: Take the 3/4-mile walk to the waterfall. There are campgrounds along the way; primitive camping in the Tenaja Trailhead area.

GETTING HOME: I-15.

MAPS: Cleveland National Forest; ACSC, *Riverside County*.

INFORMATION: Cleveland N.F., Trabuco District.

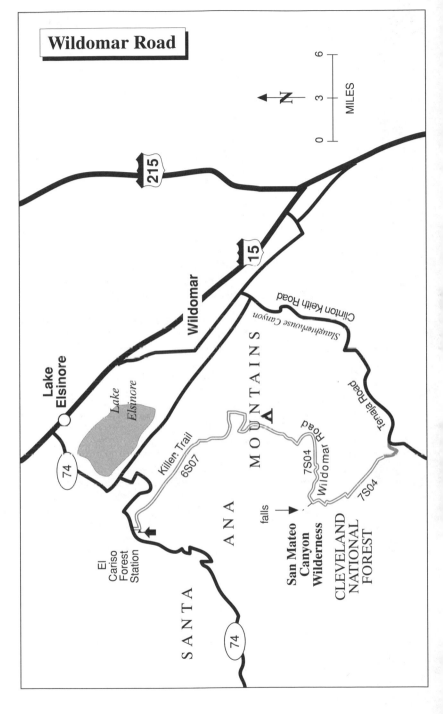

Palomar Mountain Divide

LOCATION: San Diego County northeast of Escondido. Cleveland National Forest.

HIGHLIGHTS: A gorgeous drive along a high, winding ridgeline that culminates at a fire lookout with a truly breathtaking view from 6,140 feet, the summit of a mountain that stretches for 20 miles. This drive will not get you to Palomar Observatory, but you will see it.

DIFFICULTY: Easy. Some might consider High Point Road moderate. A bit rough in spots, it is a narrow road with an intimidating drop-off on the left. You're unlikely to find anywhere to turn around easily once you start down it.

TIME & DISTANCE: 3 hours with time spent at your destination, the peak called High Point. It's 13.2 miles one-way on Palomar Divide Road to High Point. It's 14 miles from there to Highway 79 via Oak Grove & High Point roads.

GETTING THERE: Turn west onto Palomar Divide Road (9S07) off Highway 79 about 6.6 miles northwest of Warner Springs Ranch, or about 7.2 miles southeast of Oak Grove.

THE DRIVE: A sign at the entry gate says this is the only entry and exit point. Actually, one can exit via exhilarating High Point Road to make a loop. Palomar Divide Road is paved, sort of, but its tight turns and countless dips, rises and bumps will demand your full attention. The driver should save his or her sightseeing for turnouts like the one at mile 4.2, which offers a great view of Barker Valley and Lake Henshaw. Drive along steep drop-offs and climb toward the crest of the divide, which you will reach at mile 5.6. The asphalt will give way to dirt. Now the vistas are fantastic, if they aren't obscured by smog and haze. The masonry foundation near the road was the site of Ware Mine, where semi-precious stones were mined. It's private property. Continue to the fork where 9S07 goes left (west) toward High Point, and Oak Grove Road, 9S09, continues north. Take 9S07. In a mile or so is a sign directing you left up a steep track to the lookout.

REST STOPS: The lookout is a great place for lunch.

GETTING HOME: Return to Highway 79 the way you came, or descend to the highway via Oak Grove Road, 9S09, north. In 1.7 miles 9S09 will angle east but be gated off. Continue north (left) on High Point Road, 8S05.

MAPS: Cleveland N.F.; ACSC, *San Diego County.*

INFORMATION: Cleveland N.F., Palomar Ranger District.

Palomar Mountain Divide

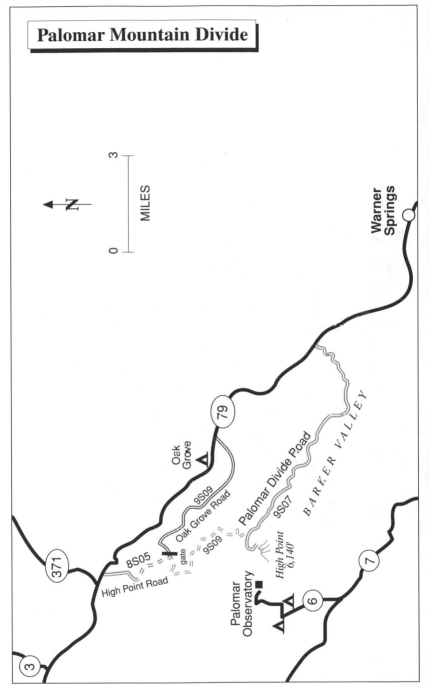

N

MILES

3

0

Warner
Springs

79

Oak
Grove

9S09

Oak Grove Road

Palomar Divide Road

9S07

BARKER VALLEY

8S05

gate

9S09

9S09

371

High Point Road

High Point
6,140'

Palomar
Observatory

7

6

3

Black Mountain Summit

LOCATION: San Diego County north of Ramona; Cleveland National Forest.

HIGHLIGHTS: Spectacular 360-degree vista from the 4,051-foot summit of Black Mountain.

DIFFICULTY: Easy to moderate.

TIME & DISTANCE: 1.5 hours; 13.8 miles round-trip. Dead-ends at the summit.

GETTING THERE: Take Pamo Road north from Ramona. When you reach the left to the landfill, keep right. The road will narrow and you will descend toward Pamo Valley. About 1.5 miles from where the pavement ends turn right (east) onto Upper Santa Ysabel Road, 12S07 on the Forest Service map. Set your odometer at 0 here.

THE DRIVE: This drive begins in pretty Pamo Valley, below 1,000 feet elevation. Then it climbs gradually on a good road that becomes increasingly narrow as it passes through chaparral, oak woodland and, near the top, conifer forest. About 1.5 miles from Pamo Road turn left (northeast) onto Black Mountain Road, 11S04 on the Forest Service map. After about 3.5 miles you will pass through a natural area that is protected for research purposes. Black Mountain Road provides fine views as it twists and winds above Organ Valley, just to the east. About 4.7 miles from where you left 12S07 Black Mountain Road is blocked by a locked gate at private property. Veer right (southeast). In about a mile you will reach the summit for sweeping views of coastal mountains and canyons.

REST STOPS: The summit, where there used to be a lookout tower.

GETTING HOME: Retrace your route.

MAPS: Cleveland National Forest; ACSC, *San Diego County*.

INFORMATION: Cleveland N.F., Palomar Ranger District.

ALSO TRY: The easy drive up to Orosco Ridge, west of Pamo Road 2.8 miles south of the turnoff to Upper Santa Ysabel Road, and follow road 12S02.

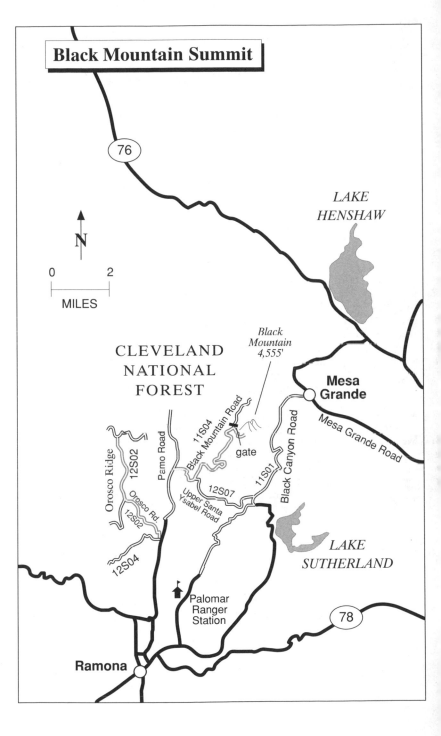

Black Mountain Summit

Black Canyon Road

LOCATION: San Diego County north of Ramona. Cleveland National Forest.

HIGHLIGHTS: Winding along the side of a deep, remote and beautiful canyon on a narrow one-lane road.

DIFFICULTY: Easy, but the road has many blind curves.

TIME & DISTANCE: An hour; 11.5 miles.

GETTING THERE: Take Main Street east through Ramona to Magnolia; turn left (north). Magnolia will eventually become Black Canyon Road. The Palomar Ranger Station is about 1.5 miles from the turn onto Magnolia. The pavement ends on Black Canyon Road after almost 1.5 miles. Set your odometer at 0 there.

THE DRIVE: Climbing gradually for 2.5 miles, you will probably lament the loss to smog of so many Southern California vistas. But you should still be able to see something of the rugged coastal valleys and mountains to the west. At mile 2.5 the road turns inland, and suddenly you're looking down into Black Canyon, at Santa Ysabel Creek, and across rolling mountain tops. Snake along the canyon wall. The road is well-maintained but narrow (use your horn on the blind curves) and the view off the edge is hair-raising. The bottom of the canyon, a stream-watered riparian area, is quite lush. At mile 4.6 cross a bridge over Santa Ysabel Creek. By 6 miles you will see many pullouts, and steep trails leading down to the rocky creek below. By mile 10.3 you've climbed to the head of the canyon. Below is Washtub Falls. Once out of the canyon the landscape becomes quite pastoral, with trees and grassy areas. By mile 11.5 you're at Mesa Grande Road, the end of the drive.

REST STOPS: Any of the pullouts along the way. Black Canyon Campground no longer exists.

GETTING HOME: Mesa Grande Road to Highway 79.

MAPS: Cleveland National Forest; ACSC, *San Diego County*.

INFORMATION: Cleveland N.F., Palomar Ranger District.

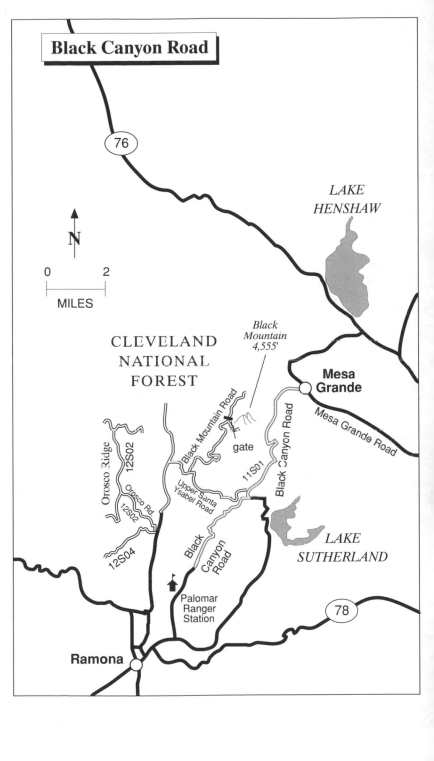

Black Canyon Road

76

LAKE HENSHAW

N

0 2
MILES

Black Mountain 4,555'

CLEVELAND NATIONAL FOREST

Mesa Grande

Black Mountain Road

Mesa Grande Road

gate

Orosco Ridge

12S02

Orosco Rd

12S02

11S01

Black Canyon Road

Upper Santa Ysabel Road

12S04

LAKE SUTHERLAND

Black Canyon Road

Palomar Ranger Station

78

Ramona

TRIP
47

Boulder Creek Road

LOCATION: San Diego County north of Descanso. Cleveland National Forest.

HIGHLIGHTS: Beautiful views to the west, from well over 3,500 feet, of fog coming in off the ocean. Rolling, chaparral-covered mountain tops strewn with granite as you drive along a winding mountain road. A relaxing scenic cruise.

DIFFICULTY: Easy on a well-maintained road.

TIME & DISTANCE: 1.5 hours; 24 miles.

GETTING THERE: On Interstate 8, take the Highway 79 exit 9 miles east of Alpine. Go north 1.6 miles to Descanso Junction, then turn left at the sign for Descanso. Go left at Perkins Store, then immediately right onto Oak Grove Drive. Soon you'll reach Boulder Creek Road, 13S08 on the Forest Service map.

THE DRIVE: One of the neat things about backcountry driving is how friendly people become when they leave the crush of highway traffic. They almost always wave when they pass. That's the way it is on this road as you wind along the western slope of the Cuyamaca Mountains. It's paved for the first 5.1 miles; then it becomes a good dirt and gravel road. By 10 miles it narrows and descends steeply into a canyon. The landscape will be more grassy, dotted with oaks. Instead of the broad vistas, the road is shady and more intimate. Cross Boulder Creek at 10.7 miles, at an improved crossing, and then start climbing out of the canyon. Once out of the canyon, the hills are more gentle and rolling, and are covered with grass and groves of hearty oaks. By mile 18 you're at Pine Hills Fire Station, and pavement resumes. To the right is Engineers Road; take it. It's a pretty drive of about 6 miles to Cuyamaca Lake and Highway 79.

REST STOPS: Perkins Store; Lake Cuyamaca (boating and fishing); Cuyamaca Rancho State Park.

GETTING HOME: Highway 79 south to I-8.

MAPS: Cleveland N.F.; ACSC, *San Diego County*.

INFORMATION: Cleveland National Forest, Descanso Ranger District; Palomar District.

Boulder Creek Road

Julian

S1

Pine Hills

Pine Hills Ranger Station

Inaja Indian Reservation

Engineers Road

13S03

13S08

Sunshine Mountain 3,041'

Mineral Hill 3,,495'

CLEVELAND

NATIONAL

FOREST

CUYAMACA LAKE

CUYAMACA RANCHO

STATE PARK

Boulder Creek Road

13S08

79

N

Descanso

0   3
MILES

8

Descanso Junction

8

Fred Canyon

LOCATION: San Diego County; Cleveland National Forest in the Laguna Mountains, part of the Peninsular coastal mountain province.

HIGHLIGHTS: A very scenic drive on a one-lane road that provides fine vistas from well over 5,000 feet elevation. East of here the relatively well-vegetated southern coast ranges fade into the hot, dry, low-lying Colorado Desert.

DIFFICULTY: Easy.

TIME & DISTANCE: An hour; about 9.8 miles.

GETTING THERE: Take the Cameron Fire Station/Kitchen Creek Road exit from Interstate 8. Follow Kitchen Creek Road north for about 4.1 miles. Turn right (east) at Cibbets Flat Campground. Follow Fred Canyon Road, 16S08 on the Forest Service map.

THE DRIVE: You will do a lot of climbing once you leave the campground and pass through Fred Canyon. The narrow roadbed consists of loose soil and small rocks, with some ruts and rocky pitches where you should use 4wd. As you pass through the chaparral-covered hills, I-8 behind you will be reduced to a thin ribbon far below. You can also look south into Baja California, Mexico. By mile 4 you're looking down into deep Antone Canyon. By mile 5.6 you can look west into pretty Long Canyon. Soon you will reach the intersection with road 15S05, on the right. Veer left (north). Pass through privately owned land, going through a couple of gates (leave them as you find them). At mile 7.1, after entering a forested area, you will enter pretty Horse Meadow. At mile 9.25 enter the Laguna Mountain Recreation Area. The paved road is another half mile or so.

REST STOPS: Cibbets Flat Campground; Laguna Mountain Recreation Area.

GETTING HOME: You'll come out on county road S1, Sunrise Highway. Take it southwest back to I-8.

MAPS: Cleveland National Forest; ACSC, *San Diego County*.

INFORMATION: Cleveland National Forest, Descanso Ranger District.

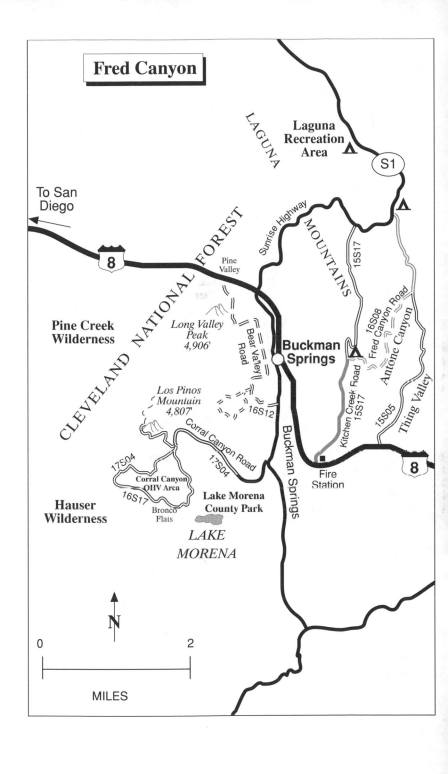

Fred Canyon

To San Diego

LAGUNA

Laguna Recreation Area

S1

8

Pine Valley

Sunrise Highway

LAGUNA MOUNTAINS

15S17

CLEVELAND NATIONAL FOREST

Pine Creek Wilderness

Long Valley Peak 4,906'

Bear Valley Road

16S08

Fred Canyon Road

Antone Canyon

Buckman Springs

Los Pinos Mountain 4,807'

16S12

Kitchen Creek Road 15S17

15S05

Thing Valley

Corral Canyon Road

17S04

17S04

Buckman Springs

8

16S17

Corral Canyon OHV Area

Bronco Flats

Lake Morena County Park

Fire Station

Hauser Wilderness

LAKE MORENA

N

0   2

MILES

Los Pinos Mountain

LOCATION: San Diego County, in Cleveland National Forest, between Interstate 8 and the Mexican border.

HIGHLIGHTS: Absolutely spectacular panoramic view that includes Mexico, the coast and the desert from a lookout tower atop a 4,805-foot peak.

DIFFICULTY: Easy.

TIME & DISTANCE: An hour and 5.1 miles round-trip, allowing time to visit with the person staffing the lookout, who can explain what you're looking at. (I've never found an unfriendly lookout staffer.)

GETTING THERE: Take the Buckman Springs exit from I-8, then Buckman Springs Road south toward Morena Lake County Park. Turn right (west) onto Corral Canyon Road, a.k.a. Morena Stokes Valley Road, and go 5.8 miles to the Corral Canyon Off-Highway Vehicle Area. You'll see Los Pinos Road, 16S17, to the right near the staging area. Set your odometer at 0.

THE DRIVE: You won't have to wait until you reach the lookout to get great vistas. The drive up has them, too. It's fairly rough and steep, but still easy. At mile 2.3 you will reach a Y; keep right. In another 0.3 miles you will be at the lookout, gazing upon rugged mountain ranges to the west, and long mesas and rolling hills to the east, where the coastal ranges give way to the sizzling, low-lying Colorado Desert. To the south, you can see well into Mexico.

REST STOPS: Corral Canyon Campground, about 1.3 miles from Four Corners, and Bobcat Meadows Campground, a mile south of the staging area at Four Corners.

GETTING HOME: I-8.

MAPS: Cleveland National Forest; ACSC, *San Diego County*. Also refer to the map on the sign at the staging area.

INFORMATION: Cleveland National Forest, Descanso Ranger District.

ALSO TRY: The easy 10.3-mile, 50-minute Bronco Flats Loop, a busy off-highway vehicle road. Refer to the map on the sign at the staging area.

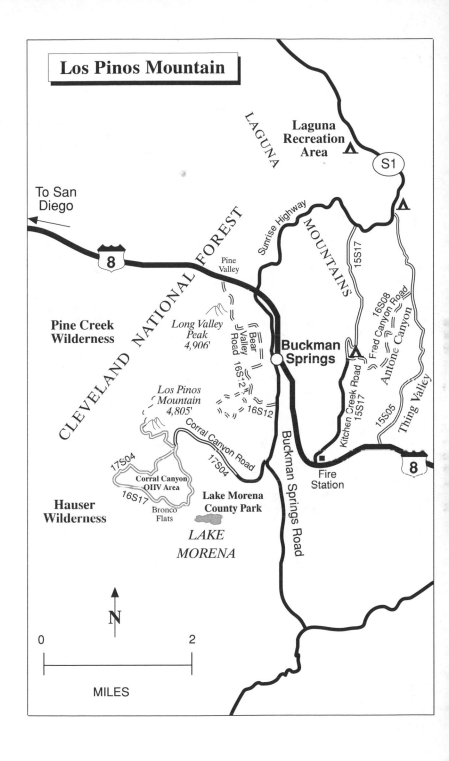

Los Pinos Mountain

Laguna Recreation Area

LAGUNA

S1

To San Diego

8

Pine Valley

Sunrise Highway

LAGUNA MOUNTAINS

CLEVELAND NATIONAL FOREST

Pine Creek Wilderness

Long Valley Peak 4,906'

Bear Valley Road 16S2T

Buckman Springs

15S17

Fred Canyon Road 16S08

Antone Canyon

Los Pinos Mountain 4,805'

16S12

Kitchen Creek Road 15S17

15S05

Thing Valley

Corral Canyon Road

17S04

17S04

Corral Canyon OIIV Area

16S17

Bronco Flats

Lake Morena County Park

Buckman Springs Road

Fire Station

8

Hauser Wilderness

LAKE MORENA

N

0   2

MILES

Bear Valley Road

LOCATION: San Diego County south of Pine Valley, on Interstate 8. Cleveland National Forest.

HIGHLIGHTS: A fun and short entry-level 4wd route with some wonderful vistas from well over 4,000 feet. On the other hand, there's a lot of litter.

DIFFICULTY: Easy to moderate.

TIME & DISTANCE: Less than an hour; 8.3 miles

GETTING THERE: Take the Pine Valley exit from I-8 about 48 miles east of San Diego. Go right at the bottom of the exit. Drive across a cattle guard, enter a paved area, keep left and you'll be on road 16S12. Set your odometer at 0.

THE DRIVE: As you will see by the spent cartridges littering this area, people are ignoring the No Shooting signs. Look beyond the litter at the chaparral-covered hills and vast panorama south to Baja California and east toward the desert and you will see why this drive is worth taking despite the litter. Parts of this drive will be somewhat rocky and rutted. At mile 4.3 go up a rise and suddenly have a spectacular view of a green valley and coastal and interior mountains. As you descend on the main road, you will get a great view of I-8 far below. What a contrast with the track you're on. In another 1.8 miles you'll reach the gate at Buckman Springs Road.

REST STOPS: Lake Morena County Park to the south.

GETTING HOME: Take county road S1, Buckman Springs Road, north to I-8.

MAPS: Cleveland National Forest; ACSC, *San Diego County.*

INFORMATION: Cleveland National Forest, Descanso Ranger District.

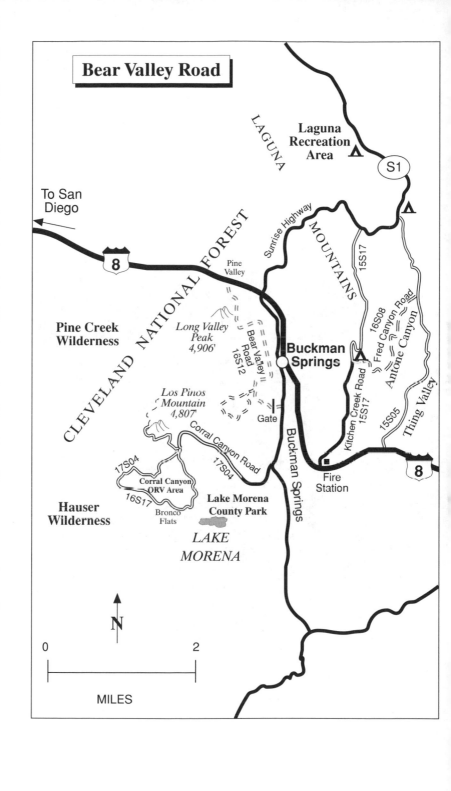

Bear Valley Road

To San Diego

Laguna Recreation Area

LAGUNA

LAGUNA MOUNTAINS

S1

Sunrise Highway

Pine Valley

CLEVELAND NATIONAL FOREST

Pine Creek Wilderness

Long Valley Peak 4,906'

Bear Valley Road 16S12

Buckman Springs

15S17

16S08

Fred Canyon Road

Antone Canyon

Los Pinos Mountain 4,807'

Gate

Kitchen Creek Road 15S17

15S05

Thing Valley

Corral Canyon Road

17S04

17S04

16S17

Corral Canyon ORV Area

Bronco Flats

Hauser Wilderness

Lake Morena County Park

Buckman Springs

Fire Station

LAKE MORENA

N

0   2

MILES

Palomar Observatory from High Point *(trip 44)*

Liebre Mountain *(trip 36)*

Trip notes

APPENDIX

Sources of information

Angeles National Forest:

Arroyo Seco Ranger District
Oak Grove Park
La Canada, CA 91011
818-790-1151

Mt. Baldy Ranger District
110 North Wabash Avenue
Glendora, CA 91740
818-335-1251

Saugus Ranger District
30800 Bouquet Canyon Road
Saugus, CA 91350
805-296-9710

Supervisor's Office
701 N. Santa Anita Avenue
Arcadia, CA 91006
818-574-1613

Tujunga Ranger District
12371 N. Little Tujunga Canyon Road
San Fernando, CA 91342
818-899-1900

Valyermo District
34146 Longview Road
Pearblossom, CA 93553
805-944-2187

Automobile Club of Southern California
Travel Publications Dept.
2601 S. Figueroa Street, H075
Los Angeles, CA 90007
213-741-4183

California Association of Four-Wheel Drive Clubs
3104 O Street #313
Sacramento, CA 95816
916-332-8890

California Department of Fish & Game
(For Eel River Wildlife Area)

619 Second St.
Eureka, CA 95501
707-445-6493

California State Automobile Association
150 Van Ness Avenue
San Francisco, CA 94102
415-565-2012

Cleveland National Forest:

Descanso Ranger District
3348 Alpine Boulevard
Alpine, CA 91901
619-445-6235

Palomar Ranger District
1634 Black Canyon Road
Ramona, CA 92065
619-788-0250

Supervisor's Office
10845 Rancho Bernardo Road
Suite 200
San Diego, CA 92127-2107
619-674-2901 or 673-6180

Trabuco Ranger District
1147 East Sixth Street
Corona, CA 91719
909-736-1811 (or 1812)

Destinet
(state park camping reservations)
1-800-444-7275

Humboldt County
707-445-7652

Los Padres National Forest:

Monterey District
406 South Mildred Ave.
King City, CA 93930
408-385-5434

Mount Pinos District
HC1
Box 400
Frazier Park, CA 93225
805-245-3731

Ojai District
1190 East Ojai Avenue
Ojai, CA 93023
805-646-4348

Santa Barbara District
HC58, Paradise Road
Santa Barbara, CA 93105
805-967-3481

Santa Lucia District
1616 Carlotti Drive
Santa Maria, CA 93454-1599
805-925-9538

Supervisor's Office
6144 Calle Real
Goleta, CA 93117
805-683-6711

Mendocino County
707-463-4363

Mil Potrero Park
805-763-4246

Monterey County
408-647-7756

Redwood Information Center
On U.S. 101 west of Orick
707-464-6101, ext. 5265

Redwood National & State Parks
Visitor Information
1111 Second Street
Crescent City, CA 95531
707-464-6101

San Luis Obispo County
805-781-5252

Santa Barbara County
805-568-3000

Sinkyone Wilderness State Park
P.O. Box 245
Whitethorn, CA 95989
707-986-7711

Six Rivers National Forest:

Supervisor's Office
1330 Bayshore Way
Eureka, CA 95501
707-442-1721
Motorized recreation
707-441-3594

Smith River National Recreation Area:
Six Rivers National Forest
Gasquet Ranger Station
P.O. Box 228
Gasquet, CA 95543
707-457-3131

Tread Lightly!
298 24th Street
Suite 325-C
Ogden, UT 84401
801-627-0077
1-800-966-9900

U.S. Bureau of Land Management
(King Range National
Conservation Area)
1695 Heindon Road
Arcata, CA 95521
707-825-2300
King Range headquarters
707-986-7731

U.S. Forest Service
Recreation Information Center
630 Sansome Street
San Francisco, CA 94111
415-705-2874

References
&
suggested reading

Looking at the scenery of California's coastal mountains but going no further is like looking at a book's cover but not reading its pages. There are stories behind the scenery. In the case of these rugged mountains, they are tales of powerful and active geology and weather, forces that continue to shape one of the world's most beautiful places.

There are scores of guides to bed & breakfast inns, romantic hideaways, hiking trails and restaurants along the coast. Check your local bookstore. I found the following books to be particularly good:

A Natural History of California, by Allan A. Schoenherr; University of California Press, 1992. Geology, flora, fauna, weather, just about everything is covered in this comprehensive (772 pages) book.

California Coastal Access Guide, by the California Coastal Commission; University of California Press, 1991 (revised). A county-by-county guide to camping, hiking, fishing, boating and many other things to do and places to go. Includes a list of coastal hostels. Anyone who spends a great deal of time exploring the coast must have one.

California Coastal Resource Guide, by the California Coastal Commission; University of California Press, 1987. A readable and detailed county-by-county tour of the coast, with descriptions of the geology, flora, fauna, regional economies and human history of the region. Many illustrations as well as black & white photographs.

California Forests and Woodlands; A Natural History, by Verna R. Johnston with drawings by Carla J. Simmons; University of California Press, 1994. Since most of the drives in *California Coastal Byways* pass through some sort of forest or woodland, you'll enjoy the drives more if you know something about what you're seeing.

California Mountain Ranges, by Russell B. Hill; Falcon Press, 1986. Gorgeous color photographs and graphics accompanied by clear, well-researched text.

Exploring the North Coast; The California Coast from the Golden Gate to the Oregon Border, by Jonathan Franks; Chronicle Books, 1996. Great historical background and current information make this a must-read for anyone setting out for the North Coast, particularly the Lost Coast.

Northern California Handbook, by Kim Weir; Moon Publications, Inc., 1994 (second edition). Another comprehensive guide that any traveler would find highly useful.

Index

Windy Point *42*

Photo index

Backcountry road signs

Maintained for passenger cars

Road number, suitable vehicle

Not maintained for passenger cars

Unsuited for passenger cars

"I want more!"

Let Tony Huegel's exciting series, *Backcountry drives for the whole family*, guide you to even more off-highway adventure. Buy these titles from your favorite bookstore, or fill out and clip this coupon — *and mail it today*!

❑ **Sierra Nevada Byways**
_____ Copies ($10.95* each)

❑ **California Coastal Byways**
_____ Copies ($18.95* each)

❑ **California Desert Byways**
_____ Copies ($18.95* each)

❑ **Idaho Off-road**
_____ Copies ($10.95* each)

❑ **Utah Byways**
_____ Copies ($16.95* each)

Idaho residents add 5% sales tax. Please include $3 for the first book ordered, and 50 cents for each additional book to cover postage and handling.

$_____ Total

Make a check or money order out to the Post Company and mail it with this coupon to:

Guidebooks
Post Company
P.O. Box 1800
Idaho Falls, ID
83403

Name: _____

Street: _____

City: _____ State: _____

Zip: _____

VISA ❑ MasterCard ❑

card number:

☐☐☐☐☐ ☐☐☐☐☐ ☐☐☐☐☐ ☐☐☐☐

Expiration date: ☐☐☐☐

Signature: _____

PHONE ORDERS: (208) 522-1800

*Prices may change without notice.